SHIPWRECKS OF THE GREAT LAKES

SHIPWRECKS OF THE
GREAT
LAKES

PAUL HANCOCK

THUNDER BAY
P·R·E·S·S

Published in the United States by
Thunder Bay Press
An imprint of the Advantage Publishers Group
5880 Oberlin Drive
San Diego, CA 92121-4794
www.advantagebooksonline.com

Produced by PRC Publishing Ltd
Kiln House, 210 New Kings Road
London SW6 4NZ

© 2001 PRC Publishing Ltd

ISBN 1 57145 291 5

Library of Congress Cataloging-in-Publication Data
available upon request.

Printed and bound in Hong Kong

1 2 3 4 5 00 01 02 03

Acknowledgements

All photographs in this book were kindly supplied
by the Milwaukee Public Library/Wisconsin Marine
Historical Society (Robert B Campbell Collection
for pages 47, 137 and 139; Ken Johnson for page
143). The photograph on page 40 (bottom) was supplied by © Layne Kennedy/CORBIS.

While some records vary, every effort has been
made to verify the facts in this book using the ship
file at the Milwaukee Public Library.

CONTENTS

Glossary

Anemometer	An instrument to measure wind velocity.
Astern	Toward the aft or rear of a vessel.
Backstays	Rigging from the mast to the stern of the vessel.
Ballast	Weight placed in or on the hull to stabilize the vessel.
Bilge	Lowest point or nearest to the keel of a vessel.
Bow	The front end of a vessel.
Boom	The lower edge of a fore-and-aft sail.
Breakers	A wave cresting while it reaches shallow water.
Centerboard	A board used to reduce the tendency for a sailing vessel to move sideways.
Chip Log	An instrument to measure a vessel's speed by towing a board from the stern over a fixed period.
Combers	Long curling waves
Course	A prearranged route that a vessel is steered.
Dead Reckoning	Determining a vessel's position from the last known sighted position.
Draft	The depth of water required for a vessel to float.
Flotsam	Wreckage from a vessel floating on the water.
Foot	The lower end of a mast or sail.
Forepeak	The extreme forward end of the bow.
Foresail	The lower sail on the foremast of a sailing vessel.
Forestay	Rigging from the mast to the bow of the vessel.
Freeboard	The distance between the deck and the waterline.
Gaff	The spar that the head and fore of a fore-and-aft sail is extended.
Gale	A strong wind categorized by its velocity from 32 to 63 mph.
Galley	The kitchen area on a vessel.
Gangway	An area on the side of a vessel to allow passengers to board and disembark from a vessel.
Gyro	A compass driven by a gyroscope that points to true north.
Harbor	An area that offers some shelter from the wind or sea.
Hatch	An opening on the deck allowing access to the hold.
Hold	The space below deck used solely for storing cargo.
Inlet	A small bay or passageway between islands or peninsulas.
Jib	A small triangular sail attached to the headstay.
Keel	The longitudinal length of the hull.
Knot	Unit of speed.
Launch	A small open boat usually with a flat bottom.
Lead	A small weight attached to a marked line used to measure depth.
League	Unit of distance equivalent to three nautical miles.
Lee	The side of shore providing shelter from the wind.
Lifelines	Metal wire supported above the deck used to prevent people from going overboard.
Lighter	A large flat bottom barge used to load or unload cargo.

Port	The left side of a vessel.
Radar	An instrument that tracks the position and size of vessels on a display.
Reef	An underwater barrier made of rock or coral.
Rigging	All the lines, stays, masts, and spars on a vessel.
Rudder	The device at or near the stern that controls the direction of a vessel.
Spar	All the masts, booms, and gaffs used in a vessel's rigging.
Starboard	The right side of a vessel.
Stern	The rear end of the vessel.
Surfboat	A small rowing boat used by United States Life Saving Service.
Tiller	An arm attached to the rudder to turn a vessel.
Ton	A unit of measure equal to 100 cubic feet of cargo capacity.
Watch	A duty period aboard a vessel usually a duration of four hours.
Wheel	A vessels steering helm or the vessel's propeller.
Yawl	A vessel's small rowing boat.

RIGHT: The *Choctaw* was wrecked on Lake Huron, July 12, 1915. See page 82.

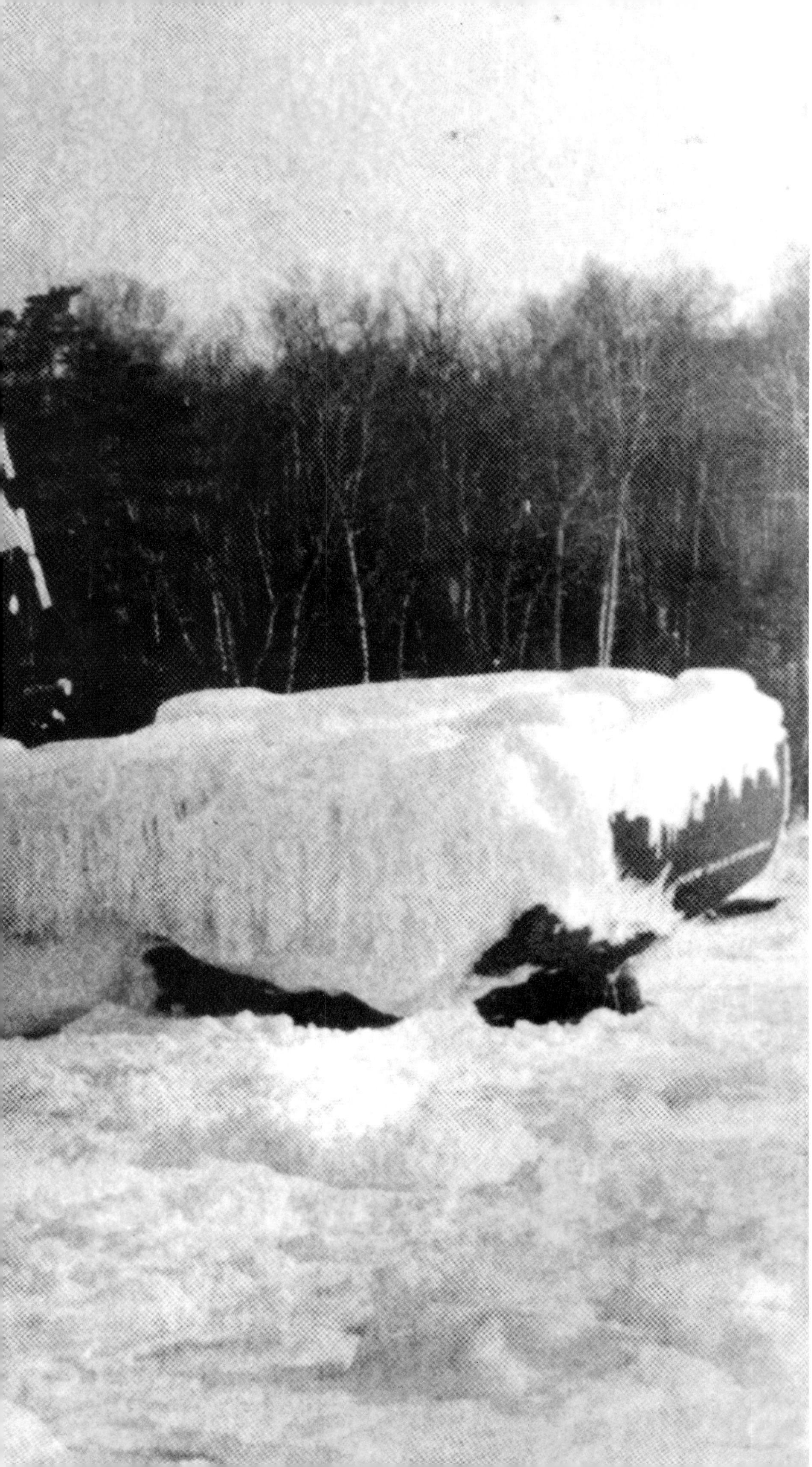

INTRODUCTION

The statistics of the Great Lakes can fill a book by themselves. These massive freshwater seas span more than 750 miles from west to east and have an area of more than 1,200,000 square miles. The lakes in the system—Superior, Michigan, Huron, Erie, and Ontario—and the minor connecting waterways between them contain nearly 18 percent of the world's fresh water. A hugely important international resource, the lakes also played a major role in the history and development of the United States and Canada.

The French were the first Europeans to discover the Great Lakes. They founded the first settlement of Montreal along the St. Lawrence River in the sixteenth century, but it was not until 1615 that the French explorers Le Caron and Champlain discovered Lake Huron and Lake Ontario. Other French explorers would discover Lake Superior (1627), Lake Michigan (1634), and Lake Erie (1669). English and Spanish explorers followed the French, much of the early exploration in search of a shorter route to the Spice Islands.

The first settlements began with the fur trade. European traders, known as "wood runners," set out in their birch canoes seeking the valuable beaver, marten, and muskrat pelts. These traders formed small outposts near river outlets to barter with the Native Americans. Eventually, private enterprise replaced the individual wood runners. By 1805, there were four companies engaged in the fur trade on the Great Lakes, the most notable being John Jacob Astor's American Fur Company, whose profits made him the richest man in North America. By 1834, however, the quantities of pelts dwindled as did demand in Europe, and much of the trade moved north to Hudson Bay or further west.

In the waning years of the fur trade, the state of New York opened the Erie Canal. Not only did this allow immigrants to travel up the Hudson River to the eastern end of Lake Erie, but opened markets to the eastern seaboard. Shortly after the Erie Canal was finished, the Canadians opened the Welland Canal between Lake Ontario and Lake Erie. The Welland provided the vital link to the markets in Montreal. By 1840, there were steamers busily shuttling immigrants along the shores of the Great Lakes. Along with passengers, new commodities such as wheat, flour, whiskey, and most importantly, lumber were being shipped across the lakes. There were enormous forests of tall white pine trees along the shores of the Great Lakes. As settlers pushed further west into the prairie states, the demand for lumber soared. By 1850, there were hundreds of lumber mills producing millions of feet of lumber each year.

By 1846, surveyors had discovered deposits of copper and iron along Lake Superior. Towns such as Marquette and Houghton were formed overnight around these huge veins of metallic ores. Additional surveys discovered gold and silver-bearing quartz along the Minnesota shoreline. Despite the great abundance of ore, it was many years before mining reached any volume. Miners along Lake Superior had limited access to lower lake ports, since vessels could not traverse the rapids along the St. Mary's River. All this changed in 1855, when the first locks opened at Sault Ste. Marie, allowing direct access for vessels to Lake Superior. This eliminated the costly practice of cargoes being unloaded, carried around the rapids, loaded again to another vessel, and only then being taken down to the lower lakes.

Meanwhile, rising emigration from Europe was filling the towns around the Great Lakes, powering the industrialization of the area. Between 1860 and 1920, cities such as Detroit, Cleveland, and Chicago became the major centers of industrial production in North America. Factories, foundries, and shops turned out gears, motors, and industrial plant. Steel became the principal commodity as the lumber industry declined after about 1880—once the seemingly endless forests had been exhausted. Vessels that once carried lumber now carried coal, iron ore, or grain. In 1860, there were over 1,000 sailing vessels around the Great Lakes, most involved in the lumber trade. By 1920, only a few schooners were still in operation.

PREVIOUS PAGE: The schooner
barge *Plymouth* shown here
after it was blown ashore on
Lake Michigan during the
Great Storm of 1913.

RIGHT: Map of the Great
Lakes. *US Army Corps of
Engineers, Detroit District*

BELOW RIGHT: Profile of the
Great Lakes. *US Army Corps
of Engineers, Detroit District*

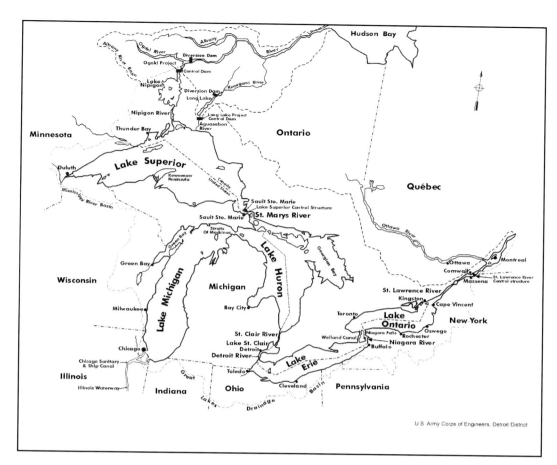

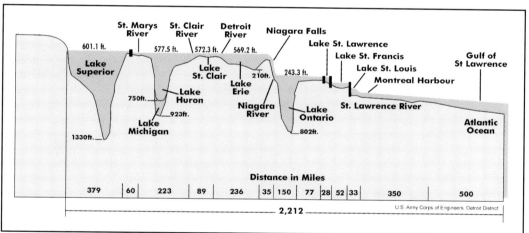

Today, the industrial centers that grew in the first half of the twentieth century have declined, partly because iron ore became more costly as the surface deposits along Lake Superior were exhausted, and partly because competition from other regions pulled people from the Great Lakes. By 1980, the Great Lakes was known as the "Rust Belt," and the decline continued. The vast fleets of vessels dwindled and there were less than a hundred ships still in operation in 1990.

One thing that has grown around the Great Lakes is the interest in the shipwrecks. Today, diving the wrecks has become a major source of entertainment for many, reflected both by the number of diving schools and diving websites. At the back of the book information is given on the divable wrecks.

GEOLOGY
The basins that are the Great Lakes are extremely young from a geological viewpoint, the result of glaciation that occurred as recently as only 11,000 years ago. Glaciers are formed as the result of long-term changes in the climate that allow snow accumulation to occur year after year. As the snow layers increase in thickness, their weight compress the snow into ice. These glaciers scoured away much of the soft erodible rock, sandstone, and

shale. They also compacted the surface by their tremendous weight as they advanced and retreated over the region.

As the last of the glaciers began to retreat from the Great Lakes region, large amounts of melt water drained into the depressed basins forming glacial lakes. Also, when the ice disappeared from the area, the land began to rebound. This rebound diverted the flow patterns of the lakes from southward through the Mississippi River valley to the north and east, where the St. Lawrence River flows today. Some 5,000 years ago, the Great Lakes' water levels dropped to the present levels.

The pinnacle of Great Lakes geology is Niagara Falls. Formed around 12,000 years ago some seven miles downstream from its present location, the falls were created by erosion of the soft shale under the harder limestone. As the shale is worn away, it takes away its support from the limestone above, which then collapses to the base of the falls. This causes Niagara to creep slowly upstream. Until the early 1950s, Niagara Falls was moving backwards at the average rate of three feet per year, before man-made water diversions slowed the rate of erosion. Today, only a fraction of the total water flow of the river goes over Niagara Falls. Much of the water is diverted into several hydroelectric power stations. Geologists have predicted that Niagara Falls will eventually change into a series of smaller rapids.

GEOGRAPHY

Lake Superior is largest of the Great Lakes. Superior measures 383 miles in length and 160 miles at its widest point, and 1,333 feet at its deepest. The major ports are Duluth, Two Harbors, Marquette, Taconite Harbor, and Superior, Wisconsin. Lake Superior received its name from the first French explorers as "*le lac superieur*"—translating as "Upper Lake." It's best known from the saying, "Superior never gives up her dead." This is actually true. Superior's cold temperature prevents bacteria growth that would cause the body to float to the surface. In many cases, bodies sink to the bottom never to be found.

Lake Michigan is the only Great Lake whose borders lie entirely in the United States. The second largest of the Great Lakes, Michigan is 321 miles in length, 118 miles wide and 932 feet at its deepest point. Large cities such as Chicago, Milwaukee, Green Bay,

and Escanaba are along its shore. Although Lake Michigan is known for its natural beauty, it was first named "Lake of the Puants" or stinking water. Not until the explorations of Marquette and Jolliet did Lake Michigan receive its final name.

Lake Huron has the highest traffic of all the Great Lakes. To the north, the St. Mary's River connects Huron to Lake Superior. To the west, the straits of Mackinaw join Lake Michigan to Huron. To the south is the St. Clair River that links Huron to Lake Erie. Huron is nearly 247 miles long, 183 miles wide, and 750 feet at its deepest point. Lake Huron includes Georgian Bay, nearly the size of a lake itself, and Saginaw Bay, that gives the State of Michigan its "thumb." Lake Huron was aptly named after the inhabitants along its shore, the Huron Indians.

Lake Erie is the shallowest of all the Great Lakes. Only 210 feet at its deepest point, Erie is 241 miles long and 57 miles wide. Notorious for its industrial pollution, it has made some efforts in the last decades to clean its environment. Yet, Lake Erie is still the industrial transportation link for the cities of Toledo, Cleveland, Buffalo, and Ashtabula on its shoreline. Lake Erie's name derives from a tribe of Indians, the Eries, along its shore. French explorers referred to Lake Erie as the "Lake of the Cat."

Lake Ontario is connected to Lake Erie in the west by two waterways. The most widely known is the Niagara River. The other is the Welland Canal. The 27-mile-long canal consists of eight locks changing in elevation by nearly 326 feet. To the east, Lake Ontario flows into the St. Lawrence River, which continues on to the Atlantic. The major ports on Lake Ontario are Toronto and Hamilton. Only 193 miles in length and 53 miles in width, Lake Ontario is the smallest of the Great Lakes. It received its name from the Iroquois word meaning "beautiful lake."

VESSELS

The first sailing vessels on the Great Lakes were skiffs and birch canoes. The earliest Europeans constructed small crafts along the shores on Lake Ontario in the 1600s. Explorers and missionaries along with fur traders extensively used such crafts. Although there were several variations, most were between 12 and 40 feet in length, with a narrow beam limited to less than six feet. They allowed access to the smaller tributaries feeding into the Great Lakes, but rarely ventured out from shore.

Merchant shipbuilding on the Great Lakes began in 1679, with the introduction of the French 70-foot *Griffon*. Similar to European designs, this vessel used the fore-and-aft rigging to give greater maneuverability in the limited space of the lakes. By 1750, there were four similar vessels on Lake Ontario. When the British took control of the Great Lakes, they built several schooners. These would be the first merchant vessels to operate on the upper lakes. For many decades these schooners engaged in the lucrative fur trade.

During the War of 1812, the lower Great Lakes' commerce ceased. Many of the earlier schooners were altered into warships. Many were poorly armed, unsuccessful in battle, and frequently not seaworthy. In 1813, the American warships *Hamilton* and *Scourge* were capsized in a storm on Lake Ontario. Many other vessels were lost to storms and canon fire. The War of 1812 resulted in a naval presence on the Great Lakes until 1949.

The prosperous period after the war reintroduced the merchant schooner. Unlike previous designs, these vessels had distinct dimensions and characteristics. The vessels were design to fit the size of the Welland Locks connecting Lake Ontario to Lake Erie. The schooners were under 100 feet long and 16 feet wide with a shallow draft. They had flat bottoms and had a centerboard to provide more stability in stronger winds. The sides were straight and were closely shaped like a canal boat. These schooners were functional, lacking the elegance of their saltwater counterparts. Many saltwater designs were used on the Great Lakes including barquentines and brigantines, but many required

larger crews or lacked the maneuverability of the schooners, of which there were over 750 sailing across the Great Lakes by 1860.

Along with schooners, steam navigation appeared on the Great Lakes after the war. These early vessels were constructed as side-wheelers. Although they were nearly 200 feet in length, many were initially slow and sometimes required sails to maintain speed. By 1840, the original steamboat design improved with the advent of the screw propellers. These vessels could traverse canals, and the machinery required less space than side-wheelers. Called "propellers," they were strengthened using iron that prevented wooden hulls from being hogged.

A new design was introduced on the Great Lakes in the 1860s—the steam barge. Steam barges, also known as "lumber hookers," were a specialized design. Most were singled-decked and fitted with a single mast similar to sailing vessels. However, they had powerful engines. While a steam barge had a capacity to carry more than a million feet of board lumber, it could tow several consort barges with similar cargo. Steam barges were a successful and efficient design for the lumber trade.

By the 1880s, a relatively small number of experimental vessels were introduced on the Great Lakes. Several used iron or a combination of iron and wood in their hulls. Although iron hulls lasted longer and were easily repaired, iron was more expensive. After iron became widely accepted, steel was introduced since it was more resilient. Both iron and steel allowed vessel dimensions to be longer and larger. Vessels grew from a mere 300 feet in 1880 to 600 feet by 1905. Unlike steam barges or propellers, these steel designs could hold large bulk cargoes and were thus aptly named bulk freight steamers.

While designers and builders adopted new materials that enabled larger tonnages and greater profits, Captain Alexander McDougall conceived several unique design concepts. The vessel had a convex deck reducing resistance to waves and winds. The pilothouse and stern cabins were atop turrets. During the 1890s nearly 40 whaleback barges and steamers were launched on the Great Lakes. Although McDougall referred to his design as whalebacks, they were commonly known as "pigboats" due to its blunt bow snout.

The prototype of modern vessels appeared on the Great Lakes by 1910. Bulk freighters incorporated safety features such as double hulls and a wireless. Other innovations changed engines from coal-fired boilers to oil or diesel motors. Ballast tanks were incorporated to add additional stability. In addition, many freighters added self-unloading booms to discharge cargo without assistance from shore.

LIGHTHOUSES AND LIFESAVERS

It is difficult today to understand the difficulties for maritime transportation on the Great Lakes in the past. Early vessels had no charts or aids for navigation, and frequently ended up stranded on an unknown shoal or foundered while seeking shelter. In these cases, sailors and passengers alike had little hope for survival since there were few settlements and their inhabitants could offer little aid.

In 1789, the U.S. Government created the Lighthouse Service and by 1819, it had established the first lighthouse on Lake Erie; others would follow quickly. These initial lights provided navigation aids around dangerous shoals and reefs. Each lighthouse was carefully watched over by a keeper and assistants. Before the advent of electricity, the keepers kept the oil burning and the lamp wicks trimmed. Many keepers described their work as mundane, and many complained of isolation. Great Lakes lighthouses differed from others since so many were built on man-made islands. The islands, better known as cribs, and towers were made of stone blocks bolted together and set in cement.

In 1837, the Congress asked the Revenue Cutter Service to begin seasonal cruises along the coast to aid mariners in distress. These cruises rarely were involved in any rescues.

As the number of shipwrecks increased, other solutions were needed to stem the problem. In 1841, the United States started a survey of the Great Lakes. Its purpose was to produce accurate navigation charts showing all the hidden reefs and shoals. The survey also included the water levels of the Great Lakes. In 1854, the United States government provided communities with surfboats to be used in rescues. These boats were to be manned by volunteers. Forty-six stations were quickly erected, but the communities received no additional equipment, only the surfboats. Normally, the boat was assigned to jurisdiction of the nearest government official, and could include customs agents, lighthouse keepers, and other minor bureaucrats. Using government officials was intended to insure proper maintenance and usage of the surfboats, but many fell in disrepair from neglect and misuse. This was brought to the attention of the public when over 200 people drowned during the winter of 1870. Direct blame was placed on the poor order of the equipment along with the untrained volunteers.

In 1875, the United States government realized that the volunteer rescue system was not working. A federal system was established as the United States Lifesaving Service. It initially established 11 stations along the Great Lakes; 19 more were added in the next few years. Each station had a man in charge, known as a keeper, who had many years of maritime experience over men and boats. His crew was selected upon a stringent examination and certification. Each man had to provide proof of his experience in handling boats as a fisherman or a wrecker. As well as submitting to a physical examination by a doctor, a candidate would have to be between the ages of 18 and 45, must live within five miles from the shores of the Great Lakes, be able to read and write English, and be a good swimmer.

Keepers were employed for a full year while the crew—the surfmen—would work only through the navigation season. During the off-season, the surfmen often found work as lumberjacks. Since surfmen were often injured during the off-season, they were required to retake a physical. There were no pensions for the injured men and no compensation for those who were killed in the line of duty.

By 1889, the Canadian Government had also established a Lifesaving Service. Initially, the Canadian service built 10 stations along the Great Lakes. After several years, additional stations were constructed. Similar to their U.S. counterparts, the Canadian service provided rescue services from Lake Superior to the St. Lawrence River.

By 1915, the Lifesaving Service joined with the Revenue Cutter Service to form the United States Coast Guard. The Canadian service joined with its navy during the same year. Both coast guard services have continued to provide rescue services along the Great Lakes. As modern navigation equipment has dramatically reduced the number of accidents of commercial vessels, the Coast Guards has focused around smaller personal crafts.

HOW TO USE THIS BOOK

This book gives details of a number of shipwrecks on the Great Lakes. Some of these were lost forever, and have never been found again; others were found but the vessels were completely written off; some were repaired and put back into service again; some were wrecked more than once. For each of the vessels listed certain basic information is provided at the end of each entry: the **Owner**, the **Builder**, the vessel's **Dimensions** in the form of length, beam, draft (all three given in feet), and gross tonnage. Finally, there are details of when the vessel was built and where. **Appendices** list all the losses in this book alphabetically, as well as divable wrecks, and a **Glossary** details maritime terms that may be unknown to the lay reader.

SHIPWRECKS

Griffon

September 18, 1679
Lake Huron

During the winter of 1679, Rene Robert Cavilier, Sieur de la Salle, began building a new vessel along the shores of the Niagara River. La Salle, like many early explorers, sought access to the wild and little known upper Great Lakes. There he hoped to accumulate furs through trade and barter and increase his personal fortune. His plan required a vessel of some size.

La Salle's ship began to take shape during the following months. The nearby white pine provided timber and iron and was forged in the wilderness, but other materials had to be shipped up Lake Ontario to the primitive shipyard. As she neared completion, the ship was also armed with seven cannon so that she could protect herself from any hostile groups that might be encountered. By August 1679, the vessel was ready to be launched and La Salle gave his new ship the name *Griffon*. A carved half eagle and half lion was placed on the bow and stern.

On August 7, 1679, the Griffon set sail. Onboard were La Salle, a friar who chronicled the voyage, several crewmen, and a Danish pilot named Luke. Luke, described as a massive man of seven feet, was an able sailor, but prone to violence and disrespect. However, he proved his skill as the *Griffon* encountered the many dangers along Lake Erie. She nearly struck Long Point and several shoals, but though Luke had no navigational aids or map to guide his way, he successfully steered her through Lake Huron and landed at Green Bay in September 1679.

La Salle engaged in trading with the local natives and amassed a full load of beaver skins, then ordered Luke and five crew to return to Niagara with the cargo. La Salle needed to reimburse his creditors and his crew, who had not been paid in over a year. He continued overland and explored the Mississippi valley. La Salle would never see his vessel again. The *Griffon* never reached Niagara. In fact, no word was heard from her after she left Green Bay.

Historians theorize that the ship navigated the islands and shoals of Lake Michigan and reached Lake Huron. There, she was struck by a fall gale, driven onto an offshore sandbar, and broke apart. However, the *Griffon*'s remains are undiscovered and the loss remains a mystery.

However, a clue to the reason for the ship's demise comes from the friar. He wrote that Luke ignored warnings from the natives of an approaching storm. With only five men onboard, a fall gale would have made the *Griffon* unmanageable. Thus, the first vessel to reach the upper Great Lakes also became their first shipwreck.

Owner: Rene Robert Cavelier, Sieur de la Salle
Builder: Moise Hillaret
Dimensions: 70.0 x 16.0 x 8.0, 60 gt.
Built: 1679 at Cayuga Creek, Niagara River

Phoenix

November 21, 1847
Lake Michigan

The propeller *Phoenix* left Buffalo, New York, on November 11, 1847, with 250 passengers on board, including many recent immigrants. Several days out, she encountered severe weather, but was able to ride out the storm. With her fuel supply low, the propeller made a stop at Manitowoc, sailing out again onto Lake Michigan on November 20. On the early morning of November 21, a fire was discovered near the engine room. It spread across the vessel rapidly, trapping most of those on board. Some 190 lives were lost in the disaster and the remains of the *Phoenix* were later towed and abandoned off Sheboygan, Wisconsin.

PREVIOUS PAGE: The carferry *Pere Marquette No. 8* burning at Marquette, Michigan, in 1927.

RIGHT: An artist's impression of LaSalle's *Griffon*—one of the first European craft to sail the western Great Lakes and the first to be shipwrecked.

Phoenix cont.
Owner: Pease and Allen
Builder: Unknown
Dimensions: 140.5 x 22.6 x 10.1, 302.9 gt.
Built: 1845 at Cleveland, Ohio

Delaware

November 12, 1855
Lake Michigan

It is the custom of vessels on the Great Lakes to recover bodies from shipwrecks. While there is no legal obligation to do so, it has long been seen as a duty and a courtesy. However, in 1847, the propeller *Delaware* outraged many local citizens when she refused to stop and recover some 30 bodies from the ill-fated *Phoenix*, which had recently burned to the waterline near Sheboygan, Wisconsin, taking over 200 lives. The weather was calm, which would have made the grim task of collecting the corpses easy, but the *Delaware*'s master wanted to continue on course. It has been suggested that he might have thought it would be bad luck to recover the dead, but whatever his motives, many people believed he simply did not care to get involved in transporting dead bodies across the lake.

On November 12, 1855, the *Delaware* sprung a leak during a severe fall storm on Lake Michigan and the deluge of water entering the holds soon overwhelmed the pumps. The vessel headed for shore, but was soon adrift and powerless after the water extinguished her boiler fires. Sailors tried in vain to hoist a small jib sail, but the *Delaware* was now at the mercy of the storm and drifted onto an offshore sandbar near Sheboygan and the master ordered the lifeboat launched with nine passengers and crew on board. The small craft start-

ed for shore, but soon capsized in the fierce weather conditions, drowning five people. The remaining crew and passengers lashed themselves to the ship to await rescue. A government lifeboat eventually saved 14 crewmen and passengers, but 11 others lost their lives to the fury of the storm. Afterward, the crew complained to the Sheboygan authorities that people on shore had robbed the dead. Ironically, they were talking of the same citizens who had complained when the *Delaware* refused to recover the *Phoenix*'s dead.

Owner: Davis and Sutton, et al.
Builder: George Davis
Dimensions: 173.1 x 24.3 x 10.3, 388 gt.
Built: 1846 at Black River, New York

RIGHT: The side-wheel steamer *Planet* was plagued with accidents until its final demise on Lake Superior in 1863.

BELOW RIGHT: The side-wheel steamer *Seabird* caught fire on Lake Michigan in 1868. There were only two survivors from the 100 people on board. (See page 22)

Lady Elgin

September 8, 1860
Lake Michigan

On September 8, 1860, the side-wheel steamer *Lady Elgin* departed Chicago bound for Milwaukee. On board were around 300 passengers who were enjoying an excursion trip across the lake. All were in high spirits even though a severe thunderstorm made the trip a rough one. Shortly after midnight, the *Lady Elgin* was struck amidships by the schooner *Augusta*, which was sailing with no running lights, and the steamer lurched over, quickly beginning to fill with water. The *Augusta* was also heavily damaged, but continued on her way to Chicago. On board the *Lady Elgin*, the master quickly turned the vessel toward shore, but the steamer only managed to limp a short distance—the damage was too severe and she soon foundered. Over 297 lives were lost in the icy waters of Lake Michigan.

Owner: Patchin, Spencer et al.
Builder: Bidwell and Banta
Dimensions: 231.0 x 33.0 x 12.0, 819 gt.
Built: 1851 at Buffalo, New York

Planet

August 1863
Lake Superior

Before navigation aids or adequate charts, vessels were in greater danger of running aground. The side-wheel steamer *Planet,* for instance, did so three times on Lake Superior within one year. In August 1862, while attempting to navigate up Portage River, she struck hard enough to cause the hull to leak. On April 30, 1863, the steamer ran aground for the second time on Portage River, but was able to free herself after several hours. A month later, she felt the ground beneath her hull again, off Fourteen Mile Point near Ontonagon, Michigan. The *Planet* finally foundered off Eagle River, Lake Superior during August 1863. Thirty-five lives were lost.

Owner: Captain E. B. Ward
Builder: J. Bushnell
Dimensions: 257.1 x 32.9 x 12.1, 1,153 gt.
Built: 1855 at Newport, Michigan

Seabird

April 9, 1868
Lake Michigan

The propeller *Seabird* was never a charmed vessel. Her first owner, E. B. Ward, placed the new ship on the Cleveland, Detroit, and Lake Superior route, and trouble first reared its head in 1860. During that year her engine sustained severe damage in an accident and had to be replaced. The following year, the *Seabird* caught fire in the Straits of Mackinaw, requiring another refit to make good the damage. By 1863, Ward had sold the ship to Goodrich Lines, which served several Lake Michigan routes. The year seemed to go well for the luckless ship until December when she ran ashore north of Milwaukee, remaining ashore until spring of 1864. After recovery she required yet more repairs. However, by 1868, the *Seabird* had finally started to make a profit, four years having passed without incident. This run of good fortune was not to last. On April 9, 1868, the propeller had left Racine with 72 passengers and crew bound for Chicago when she caught fire off Waukegan. The fire spread quickly, engulfing the *Seabird*, and forcing all aboard into the icy waters of Lake Michigan. Only two were saved when the rescuers finally arrived. Not only did Goodrich Lines suffer a vessel lost with a hefty death toll, but neither the *Seabird* or its cargo were insured.

Owner: Goodrich Lines
Builder: R. C. Conwell
Dimensions: 190.0 x 27.0 x 11.0, 444 gt.
Built: 1859 at Newport, Michigan

Globe

1873
Lake Erie

The ill-fated *Globe*, which was to be wrecked no less than three times, was originally launched as a side-wheel steamer in 1848. On November 9, 1860, the vessel's boiler exploded, and she sank in Chicago Harbor killing dockhands along with several of the crew. She was subsequently raised, her gear and machinery recovered, rebuilt, and placed back into service as a propeller. In 1863, the *Globe* met disaster again, this time in Lake Huron, when she caught fire off Big Charity Island in Saginaw Bay on August 13. The *Globe* burned to the waterline and eventually sank, but she was again raised and rebuilt into a barge. In 1873, final disaster struck the *Globe* off Leamington, Ontario, and she never sailed again

Owner: Not Listed
Builder: J. Robinson
Dimensions: 251.0 x 35.0 x 14.0, 1,233 gt.
Built: 1848 at Detroit, Michigan

Waubuno

November 22, 1879
Lake Huron

On November 21, 1879, the old side-wheeler *Waubuno* was at her dock at Collingwood, Ontario, waiting for better weather. For several days, there had been a strong gale blowing across Georgian Bay, making her intended voyage to Parry Sound impossible. However, by

RIGHT: The propeller *Globe* was first launched as a side-wheel steamer in 1848. The *Globe* was rebuilt into a propeller before ending its career as a barge in 1873.

BELOW RIGHT: The schooner *Northwest* was off Kenosha, Wisconsin, on October 26, 1876, under the command of Captain George Nedlam who was enjoying a clear fall night with good visibility. Around four o'clock in the morning, Captain Nedlam noticed the running lights of another schooner ahead—the *F. L. Danforth* carrying a full load of coal. The wind was running northwest, so the *Danforth* was close-hauled, heading north-northeast. As the two vessels came closer, the bow of the *Danforth* came around, striking the *Northwest* on the port bow and cutting deep into her hull. Seeing that disaster was imminent, Captain Nedlam quickly ordered his crew to scramble aboard the *Danforth*. The *Northwest* sank within 15 minutes of the collision, while the *Danforth* lost her jib boom, topmast, and part of her stem. Nevertheless, she was able to limp to Chicago with both crews safely on board.

BIRTHS & DEATHS

Announcement lines are open Monday to Friday 8:00 a.m. to 4:00 p.m., Saturdays 9:00 a.m. to 2:30 p.m. 6
Fax ads 605-2206. Fax deadline 2 p.m. (Deadline for next day's paper 3 p.m. previous day.)

Deaths

The Vancouver Sun notes the following deaths in today's paper

BUSTILLO	MAST
HOLLOWAY	McARTHUR
HUNTER	McAULEY
HYDE	MELEN
JONES	MILLAR
JUNAK	MOCYK
KEIGHLEY	MOUL
KENNEDY	OVANS
LEE	RUSSELL
LIN	SALVIAN
	SCHRACK
	SWALLOW
	SYMONS
	THOMAS
	THOMSON
	TROTT
	VETTERL
	WONG

Deaths

BUSTILLO — Emilio V. Bustillo Jr. Passed away July 4, 1004 at Richmond General Hospital, Richmond, aged 64 years. Predeceased by parents Emilio and Lolita Bustillo, brother Edgar Bustillo. Survived by his loving family, sisters and their husbands, Felicidad (Leonardo) Hernandez, Flordeliza (Ricardo) Sta. Maria, Millete (Cris) Pimentel; brothers and their wives, Dr. Abelardo (Lita), Ruben (Mila), Rogel, Johnny (Solly), Ramon (Faye) and sister-in-law Theresa Bustillo, many nieces and nephews, relatives and friends in Canada, USA, and the Philippines. Celebration of Life and Mass will be held at 11:30am on July 13, 2004 at St. Joseph the Worker Parish, 4451 Williams Rd., Richmond. Interment at Ocean View Burial Park.

HOLLOWAY — James peacefully in his 84th year, at Toronto East General on June 13, 2004, after a

Deaths

LIN — Prof. Paul T.K. CM
With deepest sorrow the Lin family announces the passing of Prof. Paul T.K. Lin, July 4, 2004. Born March 14, 1920, Vancouver, B.C.. Predeceased by son Christopher, and brother Dr. David Lin, sisters Mrs. Margaret Jue and and Mrs. Helen Wong. Prof. Lin will be sadly missed by his beloved and devoted wife Eileen, his loving son Dr. Douglas Lin, and three wonderful grandchildren, Jane, Edward and Albert Lin, and his brother Andrew and sister-in-law Pearl Sun Lin.
Among the many honours and positions Prof. Lin held were: The Order of Canada in 1998, the Soong Ching Ling Honorary Camphor Tree Award by the China Welfare Institute in 2003, Honorary Professor, and

Deaths

MILLAR — Terrence Arthur (Terry) passed away in his sleep at Lions Gate Hospital in North Vancouver early on the morning of July 7, 2004 after a lengthy battle with cancer. Terry was born in Lions Gate Hospital on August 17, 1941; he grew up in North and West Vancouver and later moved to Port Moody, BC. Terry was an avid sports enthusiast and golfer. He owned and enjoyed thoroughbred horses, fishing and walking in the woods. He is survived by his wife Jackie, son Geoff (Ingrid), mother Grace, sister Katherine and two grandchildren. A private celebration of life will be held at Gary and Lynne's home on the afternoon of Saturday, July 10, 2004. In lieu of flowers, donations may be made to the Royal Canadian Legion or to the Canadian Cancer Society.
Hollyburn Funeral Home (604-922-1221)

MOCYK — Wasyl (Bill)
Has peacefully started the next part of his journey on July 3rd, 2004 and was predeceased by his wife Gertrude on October 15, 2003. He was born on May 2nd, 1920, in Buczacz, Ukraine and came to Vancouver in 1954. He will be sorely missed by his, 2 children Irene Kitura and John Mocyk. and 2 grandchildren Stephanie and Elizabeth Kitura. He is also survived by many nieces and nephews in the Ukraine. A mass will be celebrated at 10 am on July 12th, 2004 at St. Mary's Ukrainian Catholic Church, 550 West 14th Avenue, Vancouver, BC. Basilian Fathers presiding. In lieu of flowers, donations to the Diabetes Foundation or the Heart and Stroke Foundation would be greatly appreciated. The family would also like to thank Dr. David Thomson and the

Deaths

SYMONS — Jo
peacefully on S
battle with canc
with dignity. He
daughter Janet,
Kevin and Ian D
David Symons o
nephews; and
beloved wife Vi w
Lower Mainland,
was born in 1920
Kitsilano Boys Ban
High School, and
that nurtured
development of me
participation in mu

Ship-shape, but with the wind out of her sails

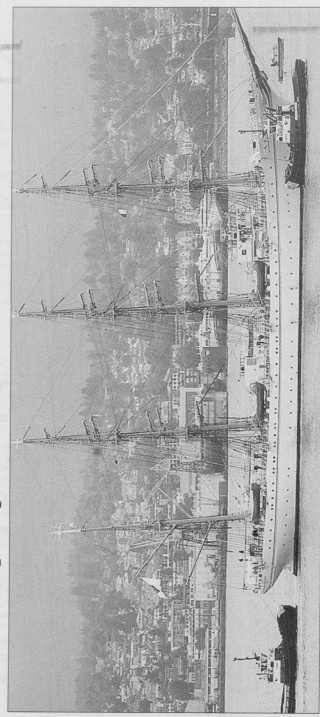

BILL KEAY/VANCOUVER SUN

The Kaiwo Maru, a Japanese sail-training vessel, is escorted by tugs into Vancouver harbour Thursday. The ship sails to Richmond July 13 and on July 14 cadets will demonstrate a sail drill, climbing the ship's 55-metre masts to lower and raise the ship's sails.

LEFT: The small paddlewheel steamer *Waubuno* before its upturned hull was discovered in 1879.

BELOW LEFT: The side-wheel steamer *Alpena* vanished on Lake Michigan in 1880 with the loss of 60-86 lives.

BOTTOM LEFT: The steamer *Asia* sank on Lake Huron in 1882. Of the passengers and crew, only two people survived the disaster.

early morning on November 22, the weather had improved sufficiently to depart and the *Waubuno* headed out from Collingwood. Her route to Parry Sound was treacherous, with many islands, reefs, and narrow passages to navigate. Adding to the difficulties of an already dangerous voyage, the gale intensified soon after departure and visibility was limited. Unable to navigate, the vessel struck a reef and was soon pounded to pieces against the rocks. The hull of the *Waubuno* was found on November 24, off Moose Point, but the bodies of the 24 people, including crew and passengers, were never recovered.

Owner: William Beatty
Builder: M. Simpson
Dimensions: 135.0 x 19.0 x 7.0, 465 gt.
Built: 1865 at Thorold, Ontario

Alpena

October 16, 1880
Lake Michigan

The fate of the wooden steamer *Alpena* has caused great speculation. On October 15, 1880, she left Grand Haven for Chicago, passing by another steamer, *Muskegon,* at around one o'clock in the morning. Other vessels also sighted the *Alpena* later on October 16, but she never arrived in Chicago. The only clue to her fate was wreckage that came ashore at Holland, Michigan. Some authors have theorized that the steamer encountered a tornado that led to her sinking, but it is more likely that waves opened her seams and she slowly sank as water filled her holds. The only thing of which we can be certain is that the *Alpena* foundered, taking all aboard her. Even the number of lives lost to this mysterious incident vary—conflicting reports state that anywhere from 60 to 86 people were aboard when she was lost.

Owner: Goodrich Lines
Builder: Gallagher
Dimensions: 197.0 x 26.0 x 12.0, 653 gt.
Built: 1866 at Marine City, Michigan

Asia

September 14, 1882
Lake Huron

The small propeller *Asia* was bought by the North Western Transportation Company in 1882 as a replacement for the owner's other propeller, *Manitoulin,* which had burned the previous May. The *Asia* was placed into service on Georgian Bay where her shallow draft allowed her to haul freight and passengers between the many small communities to Sault Ste. Marie.

On the night of September 13, 1882, the *Asia* was busily loading passengers and freight at Owen Sound, Ontario. All the cabins were occupied and some of the 125 onboard had to find a corner of the deck to sleep on. A young Duncan Tinkiss along with his uncle were fortunate to have one of the warm cabins. Down the passageway in another was another teenager, Miss Christine Morrison. She had just missed boarding another vessel, but was able to book passage on the Asia at the last moment. Miss Morrison's cousin, John McDonald, was the *Asia*'s first mate and used his influence to reserve a room for her.

While the passengers were getting settled for the night, the ship's crew were hastily throwing cargo onto the deck. Crates, bales, and other freight were strewn across the deck. Down in the hold were several teams of workhorses and cattle destined for lumber camps and farms.

The Asia's master, Captain John Savage, knew the passage from Owen Sound to French River and then to Sault Ste. Marie was going to be rough. There had been a strong wind all day and there were warnings of an approaching storm. Captain Savage talked with the owners about the worsening conditions, but the *Asia*'s route only exposed the propeller for a few miles from a sheltered shoreline. After some discussion, they agreed to let the *Asia* set sail.

Just after midnight, Captain Savage steered the *Asia* away from the Owen Sound docks and headed up the Bruce Peninsula. In just a short time, the vessel began to roll. Clearly, the propeller was top heavy from the large amounts of cargo on deck. Captain Savage decided to take on additional fuel of cordwood at Gravelly Bay, hoping the additional weight would provide the necessary ballast to stabilize the ship.

During the early morning, the *Asia* proceeded up the Bruce Peninsula and eventually entered the unprotected waters connecting Georgian Bay with Lake Huron. There she was struck by mountainous waves that rushed over her deck. Captain Savage struggled to keep the *Asia* on course as the wind and waves pushed the vessel precariously into the trough, but she was still top heavy and Captain Savage knew he needed to lighten his vessel of the cargo on deck. Accordingly, he ordered First Mate McDonald to dump all the boxes and crates still lashed to the deck overboard.

By eight o'clock in the morning, the *Asia* was still struggling to cross the open water as the heavy weather reduced her speed. A few passengers attempted to eat breakfast, but even the heartiest were seasick. But, even with the ship still rolling with each wave, all onboard were confident that Captain Savage and the *Asia* would reach the French River safely.

At 11 a.m., the storm increased in ferocity and the pounding became too much: the *Asia* slipped into the troughs. Suddenly, she rolled violently on her beam ends, nearly capsizing. Frightened passengers rushed up on deck. It was plain that the *Asia* was lost and everyone wanted to escape to the three lifeboats onboard, but the crew knew the lifeboats would be quickly smashed if they were lowered while the vessel was still rolling. However, it made little difference when the stern lurched downward and broke away from the rest of the vessel. Within seconds, everyone was tossed into the churning water.

Those passengers in the icy water quickly perished. Young Duncan Tinkiss found himself in the water next to a lifeboat. He clambered in, but he soon realized that the

BELOW: The wooden steamer *Manistee* foundered somewhere on Lake Superior with all hands in 1883.

lifeboat offered little protection. Frightened passengers climbing into the same lifeboat soon caused it to become swamped and Tinkiss felt he had better chances in another lifeboat, which he sighted in the floating debris. He jumped overboard and swam with all his strength to the other boat and, fortunately, reached it and was pulled onboard. In the lifeboat with Tinkiss was Miss Morrison, mate McDonald, Captain Savage, and 14 other passengers.

Although the lifeboat had airtight chambers preventing it from sinking, the waves soon capsized it several times. After each capsizing, fewer and fewer were able to climb back onboard. Tinkiss and Morrison decided to conserve their strength and stay in the water, holding onto to ropes attached to the bow and stern of the lifeboat. As the hours passed, the storm abated, but now there were only seven survivors remaining. During the night, they began to succumb to the cold. Two burly lumberjacks were first to perish, and a few hours later a passenger who had almost missed the *Asia* died, to be followed by Mate McDonald and Captain Savage. Miss Morrison and Duncan Tinkiss, however, remained alive in the drifting lifeboat.

The next morning brought some hope to the two young survivors. The weather was clear, sunlight offered some warmth, and a slight breeze pushed the lifeboat to a rocky island. Tinkiss and Morrison were overjoyed. Weak and exhausted, they looked for food and any available help. After a search of the island they realized that it was devoid of any human occupants and famished, they collected the only food they could find, small berries.

After two days on the island, the two young survivors came across a Native-American couple who had sailed over to the small island. They pleaded to take them to the nearest town and the next day Duncan Tinkiss and Miss Morrison arrived at Parry Sound, Ontario. After some food and rest, both recovered from their ordeal.

The remainder of the crew and passengers did not survive. Over 100 lives were lost when the *Asia* foundered, making it one of the worst disasters on the Great Lakes.

Owner: Captain Fred Burke et al.
Builder: M. Simpson
Dimensions: 136.0 x 23.4 x 11.0, 613 gt.
Built: 1873 at Welland Canal

Wells Burt

May 21, 1883
Lake Michigan

The *Wells Burt* was sailing from Buffalo to Chicago with a load of coal when she encountered a furious spring gale, off Evanston, Illinois. The ship's steering gear failed and the schooner fell into the trough of the heavy seas, waves washing across her decks and pouring into the holds. Waterlogged, she sank, taking the lives of all 11 crewmen on board. The *Wells Burt* was written off as a total loss since salvaging the schooner was impossible.

Owner: Dunham and Mosher
Builder: Detroit Dry Dock Company
Dimensions: 201.0 x 33.5 x 14.2, 756 gt.
Built: 1873 at Detroit, Michigan

Manistee

circa November 16, 1883
Lake Superior

The passenger and freight propeller *Manistee* arrived at Bayfield, Wisconsin, on the morning of November 11, 1883, just as a strong fall gale blew in across Lake Superior. She stayed in

Bayfield for the next several days awaiting more clement weather. Late in the night of November 15, the winds died down and the *Manistee* departed for Ontonagon, Michigan. When the ship failed to arrive there, speculation about the propeller's whereabouts began. By November 20 the first wreckage floated ashore along the Keweenaw Peninsula—a rudder, tables, chairs, buckets, foodstuffs, and parts of the vessel—leaving no doubts that the *Manistee* had foundered. Along with six passengers, a crew of 24 perished in the wreck.

Owner: Engelmann Transportation Company
Builder: E. M. Peck
Dimensions: 155.1 x 27.0 x 10.0, 561 gt.
Built: 1867 at Cleveland, Ohio

RIGHT: Lithograph of the *Wells Burt*. The schooner would founder with all hands on Lake Michigan in 1883.

BELOW RIGHT: The passenger steamer *Algoma* was built in Scotland and had to be cut in two and reassembled to pass through the Welland Canal.

Erie Belle

November 21, 1883
Lake Huron

The tug *Erie Belle* exploded on November 21, 1883, at Kincardine, Ontario, where she had been sent to pull free the stranded schooner *J. N. Carter*. Unfortunately, her boiler could not withstand the strain of the operation and burst. The reason for the explosion was clear to investigators: the chief engineer had altered the boiler's maximum steam pressure from that set by inspectors. The tragic result was a twisted mass of metal and four crewmen dead.

Owner: Odette and Wherry
Builder: Jenkins Brothers
Dimensions: 112.0 x 20.0 x 9.0, 292 gt.
Built: 1862 at Windsor, Ontario

Algoma

November 7, 1885
Lake Superior

The steel passenger steamer *Algoma* was too long to fit through the Welland Canal connecting lakes Erie and Ontario, and was cut in two and reassembled in Montreal during 1884. The engineering work was successful, but fate decreed that *Algoma* would again be broken in two—although next time under very different circumstances. On November 5, 1885, she left Owen Sound, Ontario, bound for Port Arthur. After locking through the "Soo," the *Algoma* encountered a typical fall gale. Throughout the day and continuing into the night, the gale increased and visibility dropped until the crew could barely see the bow of the vessel from the pilothouse. Under these conditions, the *Algoma* struck the south shore of Isle Royale, where the waves punished the steamer until the bow section broke off and sank. The steamer was declared a total wreck. Of the 62 souls aboard her at the time, only 24 survived.

Owner: Canadian Pacific Railroad
Builder: Aiken and Mausell
Dimensions: 262.15 x 38.25 x 23.2, 1,773 gt.
Built: 1883 at Glasgow, Scotland

City of Green Bay

October 3, 1887
Lake Michigan

The life of the schooner *City of Green Bay* proved to be difficult and short right from her launch when she slid only about halfway down the drydocks before getting stuck. A few days later a second attempt was arranged, with a tug on hand to provide additional persuasion, and the ways were lubricated, but before everything was ready the schooner slid off into the water. This inauspicious beginning was only one of many unusual incidents in the *City of Green Bay*'s lifetime. In 1881, she collided with another schooner off Chicago; in 1882, she ran aground on South Fox Island on Lake Michigan; in 1886, she again collided with another vessel on Lake Michigan. Each time the ship was recovered and repaired.

However, on October 3, 1887, she would not be so fortunate. She left Escanaba, Michigan, heavily laden with pig iron for St. Joseph, Michigan. The weather was moderate at first, but the wind graually increased from the west and by midnight the ship was caught in a howling gale. The *Green Bay* labored heavily through the ferocious weather, but began to take on water. By the time South Haven Light was sighted, there was five feet of water in the holds. The master decided to turn his vessel toward shore, but only struck an offshore bar. The waves drove the schooner broadsides till it grounded 600 feet from shore with surf erupting over her,

BELOW: The five-masted schooner *David Dows* was the largest sailing vessel seen on the Great Lakes. When the *Dows* was turned into a tow barge, she still kept her unique five masts.

forcing the crew up into the rigging. The lifesaving service made several attempts to rescue the crew, but the waves were too high. Eventually, the masts gave way and the men were swept into the surf. Only one survived the final voyage of the *City of Green Bay*.

Owner: Parker et al.
Builder: Christianson
Dimensions: 145.0 x 25.0 x 11.0, 346gt.
Built: 1872 at Green Bay, Wisconsin

David Dows

November 29, 1889
Lake Michigan

With a keel over 260 feet long, the *David Dows* has the distinction of being the largest schooner ever to sail the Great Lakes. She was also the only schooner to have five masts. Her owners banked on the idea that a larger vessel would increase cargo capacity, and thus turn greater profits. In fact, the *David Dows'* size caused great difficulties: she could not be loaded to capacity since her draft would be too great to enter most harbors, and even with her five masts she proved to be much slower and harder to maneuver than a smaller schooner. Although she was a grand spectacle to witness, in 1883—only two years after her launch— the *Dows* was cut down to a tow barge.

On November 29, 1889, the *Dows*, under the tow of the steamer *Aurora*, encountered gale-force winds and began to take on water. Her pumps could not hold back the flood, and she foundered off Chicago. The crew sought safety up in the masts and rigging and waited out the storm. The following day, they were rescued by the tug *Chicago*; although some would lose limbs to frostbite, no lives were lost. Salvagers removed much of the *Dows'* woodwork and gear before the Coast Guard dynamited the wreck as a potential hazard to shipping.

Owner: M. D. Carrington
Builder: Bailey Brothers
Dimensions: 275.0 x 37.6 x 18.1, 1,418 gt.
Built: 1881 at Toledo, Ohio

Two Fannies

August 8, 1890
Lake Erie

On August 8, 1890, eight exhausted men and a pet cat were pulled aboard the tug *James Amadens*. The men were the crew of the schooner *Two Fannies,* which had foundered earlier that night. The ship had been caught in a storm during which her hull sprang a leak. Despite the crew's best effort, water had risen faster and faster until the vessel was completely water-logged and the crew was forced to abandon ship in the lifeboat. After several hours of rowing toward shore, a nearby steamer signaled a tug to their rescue. The schooner was declared a total loss.

Owner: A. Miller et al.
Builder: Spears
Dimensions: 152.0 x 33.0 x 12.8, 492 gt.
Built: 1862 at Peshtigo, Wisconsin

Western Reserve

August 30, 1892
Lake Superior

On August 30, 1892, the steel steamer *Western Reserve* broke in two off Whitefish Point, Lake Superior. The vessel was battling a storm when a crash was heard by the crew. A large crack appeared across the deck, extending down the sides of the hull, and those aboard scrambled to the stern just as the steamer broke in two. While they escaped in the two lifeboats, the *Western Reserve* lurched over and sank. Sadly, the crew and passengers were not to find safety aboard the lifeboats. As they approached the shoreline, large breakers capsized them spilling everyone into the water. Only one crewman with a life preserver was able to stay afloat and reach shore alive. The other 26 crew and passengers struggled in the surf to no avail. Their bodies were recovered later.

Owner: P. G. Minch et al.
Builder: Cleveland Shipbuilding Company
Dimensions: 300.7 x 41.2 x 21.0, 2,392 gt.
Built: 1890 at Cleveland, Ohio

RIGHT: The schooner *Two Fannies* was heavily damaged on Lake Michigan in 1879.

BELOW RIGHT: This is a rare photograph of the steamer *Western Reserve* before she mysteriously broke in two on Lake Superior.

Guiding Star

August 31, 1892
Lake Superior

Vessels along the Great Lakes frequently salvage gear and equipment from other ships for their own use, so when the *Guiding Star* was being constructed in 1867, it was not considered unusual that her boiler was taken from the former propeller *Kentucky*. However, the decision to acquire an old boiler would bring disaster on July 17, 1870. The *Guiding Star* was docked at Port Maitland, Ontario, when her boiler exploded killing seven crewmen. The explosion was so terrific that her upper works completely disintegrated.

The vessel was rebuilt as a schooner in 1871 and served until August 31, 1892, when the *Guiding Star* was driven ashore near Big Bay Point, Michigan, during a fall gale. She was declared a total loss.

Owner: Joe Nicholson
Builder: D. Lester
Dimensions: 164.0 x 27.0 x 12.0, 384 gt.
Built: 1867 at Marine City, Michigan

W. H. Glitcher

October 28, 1892
Lake Michigan

No one knows exactly what happened to the steel steamer *W. H. Glitcher*. She was bound for Milwaukee on October 28, 1892, but foundered with all 27 hands en route. What had caused the new steamer to sink? One theory is that the *Glitcher* collided with another vessel. This is supported by the fact that the wreckage from the *Glitcher* was found caught up with debris from the schooner *Ostrich*, which disappeared near the same location. Another theory suggests that the *Glitcher* broke in two, backed up by the fact that the *Glitcher's* sister ship, the *Western Reserve*, had foundered due to structural failure only two months

previously. Following the tragedy questions were raised as to the quality of steel used in the construction of both steamers.

Owner: J. C. Gilchrist
Builder: Cleveland Shipbuilding Company
Dimensions: 301.5 x 41.2 x 21.1, 2,414 gt.
Built: 1891 at Cleveland, Ohio

Zach Chandler

October 29, 1892
Lake Superior

The schooner-barge *Zach Chandler* was blown ashore on October 29, 1892, on Lake Superior. She was bound for the "Soo," under tow from the steamer *John Mitchell* when the towline broke, leaving the ship powerless against the storm. The schooner attempted to raise her sails, but each was torn to shreds by high winds. Heavy seas pushed the vessel until she struck a sand-bar some 300 yards offshore. Five crewmen escaped into the lifeboat and reached shore safely, while the remaining two crewmen and the master attempted to save themselves on a makeshift raft. One man lost his grip and drowned, but the master and the other crewman were pulled ashore by the Deer Park Lifesavers. The *Zach Chandler* disintegrated.

Owner: Palmer et al.
Builder: James M. Jones
Dimensions: 194.0 x 35.6 x 14.3, 726 gt.
Built: 1867 at Detroit, Michigan

John B. Merrill

October 14, 1893
Lake Huron

As the schooner *John B. Merrill* pulled away from the docks at Buffalo, the master's wife's pet, a black cat, abandoned ship by jumping from the vessel to the dock—a distance of nearly ten feet. Some of the *Merrill*'s crew were amazed that the cat had successfully leaped across such a gap, while others remarked that it was a sign of bad luck. They were to be proved right, though the fate that awaited the ship could have been a lot worse. On October 14, 1893, while carrying a cargo of coal, the schooner was run aground on Holdridge Shoal, Lake Huron, by a strong fall storm. In spite of the bad omen, her fortunate crewmen were all saved by nearby Drummond Island fishermen. While the *John B. Merrill* broke up and was declared a total loss, not a single life was lost.

Owner: Connelly Brothers
Builder: Allan McClelland and Company
Dimensions: 189.0 x 34.0 x 13.3, 640 gt.
Built: 1873 at Milwaukee, Wisconsin

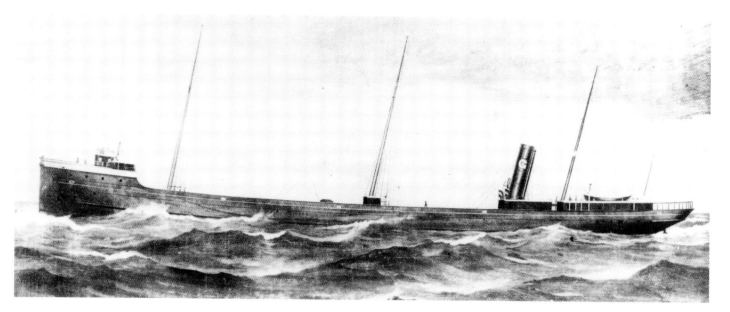

ABOVE: *W. H. Glitcher.*

Albany and *Philadelphia*

November 7, 1893
Lake Huron

Heavy fog resulted in the loss of two vessels on November 7, 1893. In conditions of extremely low visibility, the passenger steamer *Albany*, bound for Buffalo from Milwaukee with a cargo of grain, collided with the merchant steamer *Philadelphia* northeast of Point Aux Barques, Lake Huron. After the impact, both vessels were severely damaged and began to take on water. The *Albany* was the first to sink, and all crew crossed to the *Philadelphia*. However, the latter was quickly going under too, and was soon abandoned in her turn. Eight lives were reported lost from the *Albany* after a lifeboat filled with her casualties failed to make the shore, while the *Philadelphia* lost 16 in similar circumstances. Following the incident the crew of each ship blamed the other for the tragedy, though evidence suggests that both vessels had been traveling too fast for the conditions.

Owner: Western Transit Company
Builder: Detroit Dry Dock Company
Dimensions: 267.0 x 38.5 x 13.8, 1,917 gt.
Built: 1884 at Wyandotte, Michigan

Chicora

January 21, 1895
Lake Michigan

On January 1, 1895, the *Chicora* was laid up for winter, her furniture, carpet, and items from the cabins stored ashore. However, she was placed back in service on January 15 to deliver a shipment of flour. On the morning of January 21, the *Chicora* was fully loaded in Milwaukee and headed out onto the lake, bound for Ludington, Michigan. She left before the arrival of a last-minute telegram from Graham and Morton saying that the *Chicora* should wait in Milwaukee for a storm to pass. The message failed to reach the ship in time and, unsuspecting, she left harbor. By the afternoon the weather had shifted from a brisk breeze to a furious gale, with winds gusting up to 64 mph, and the temperature dropping 23 degrees. The *Chicora* was caught in the middle of the lake when the gale struck, and was never sighted again, taking all of the 30 lives aboard her. Evidence of the *Chicora*'s fate was indicated by wreckage that floated ashore near South Haven.

Owner: Graham and Morton Transportation Company
Builder: Detroit Dry Dock Company
Dimensions: 198.5 x 35.0 x 13.6, 1,122 gt.
Built: 1892 at Detroit, Michigan

STEAMER CHICORA

ABOVE: After the great 1871 fire, the city of Chicago introduced the use of fireboats. The *Yosemite* was the third owned by the city and had the ability to pump over 6,500 gallons of water a minute. On September 13, 1894, the *Yosemite* sank off South Chicago on Lake Michigan. The fireboat would be later raised and repaired.

LEFT: The steamer *Chicora* pictured with members of its crew. The *Chicora* sank somewhere on Lake Michigan during a violent storm in 1895. (See page 35)

ABOVE RIGHT: *John B. Merrill.* (See page 34)

RIGHT: The steamer *Albany* was used in the package freight trade between Buffalo, Milwaukee and Chicago. The steamer *Philadelphia* struck the *Albany* in heavy fog on Lake Huron in 1893. (See page 35)

Idaho

November 6, 1897
Lake Erie

The package freight and passenger steamer *Idaho* foundered off Long Point, Lake Erie, on November 6, 1897, after leaving Buffalo, bound for Milwaukee, with a cargo of general merchandise. By late evening, the *Idaho* was caught in a fall gale and her master decided to seek safety, but the ship needed to turn around 180 degrees for Long Point, the nearest shelter. While completing the turn, the steamer fell precariously into the trough of the seas and waves washed over her decks, sweeping six crewmen overboard. Waves also rushed into the engine room, extinguishing the boiler fires. The steamer was now without power and at the mercy of the gale. Of the 21 men aboard, 19 would perish. The fortunate pair that were rescued had lashed themselves to a spar from which they were plucked in mountainous seas by the steamer *Mariposa*.

Owner: Western Transportation Line
Builder: Peck and Masters
Dimensions: 220.5 x 32.0 x 12.3, 1,110 gt.
Built: 1863 at Cleveland, Ohio

Northwest

April 6, 1898
Lake Michigan

On April 6, 1898, the propeller *Aurora* and her tow, the schooner *Northwest,* were near St. Helena Island Light when the *Northwest* struck a submerged icefloe. Immediately, the schooner began to take on water. The *Aurora* changed course and headed for shallow water hoping to save the stricken ship, but the effort was in vain. Since much of Lake Michigan was choked with icefloes, the vessel's path was blocked. Unable to reach safety in time, the *Northwest* sank, although her crew managed to escape to the *Aurora* with no loss of life. Both vessels were carrying corn from Chicago bound for Buffalo.

Owner: James Corrigan and John Huntington
Builder: Theophilus Boston
Dimensions: 223.3 x 37.5 x 15.0, 1,017 gt.
Built: 1873 at Bangor, Michigan.

L. R. Doty

October 23, 1898
Lake Michigan

The *L. R. Doty* left Chicago on October 22, 1898, her hold filled with a cargo of corn. As many times before, she was towing her consort, the schooner-barge *Olive Jeanette*. Their progress was slow, and on Tuesday the 23rd, a strong fall gale caught the two ships off Milwaukee. As the gale gained in intensity, the *L. R. Doty* dropped the towline to the *Olive Jeanette,* leaving the latter to fend for herself. The *L. R. Doty* continued on, heading north into the mounting waves. All day Wednesday the gale raged across the lakes while many steamers stayed safely in port. Not until Thursday the 25th did the gale blow itself out. The *Olive Jeanette* was sighted near Racine, still afloat, though with her sails and rigging torn and water in her hold, but

RIGHT: In theory, the *Idaho* could use sails from the large mast behind the pilothouse to propel the steamer in case of engine failure. On the night of November 6, 1897, the theory was put to the test, but the storm that had extinguished the boiler fires proved too much and she foundered.

the *L. R. Doty* had disappeared from sight. Inquires were sent out to see if she had taken shelter or was stranded on some isolated shore. When all returned negative, hope faded that she and her crew had survived the gale, but not until the tug *Prodigy* arrived in Chicago with wreckage from the *Doty* was her fate known for sure—she had foundered off Milwaukee some time during the night of the 23rd, taking the lives of her 17 crew and her master, Christopher Smith.

Owner: W. A. Hawgood
Builder: F. W. Wheeler and Company
Dimensions: 291.0 x 41.0 x 19.8, 2,056 gt.
Built: 1893 at West Bay City, Michigan

Fedora

September 20, 1901
Lake Superior

Fedora was completed in 1889 at a cost of $125,000. She bore the same name as a famous stage play of the era and was officially christened by the show's star, Fanny Davenport. The ship, built of oak and iron, was something of a giant, with four masts, two decks, a 20-foot hold, and a tonnage of 1,849. Her final voyage was a routine trip that turned to chaos when a kerosene lamp exploded in the engine room and set fire to the ship. The captain beached the blazing vessel at Chicago Beach, north of Buffalo Bay, and the crew escaped in lifeboats while the ship burned. The following day the *Ashland Daily Press* reported the wreck "a most gruesome sight indeed." Thereafter, it became a popular excursion for sightseers.

ABOVE: The steamer *L. R. Doty* foundered on Lake Michigan during a fall gale in 1898. She is shown here at the Soo Locks.

RIGHT: The wreck of the *Fedora* became a popular excursion for sightseers.

Owner: Great Lakes Steamship Company
Builder: F. W. Wheeler
Dimensions: 282.0 x 41.0 x 20.0, 1849 gt.
Built: 1889 at West Bay City, Michigan

Bannockburn

November 21, 1902
Lake Superior

The steamer *Bannockburn* was built in the finest traditions at Middlesbourgh, Scotland, in 1893. Her dimensions allowed the ship to traverse the complete length of the Great Lakes, and, despite the occasional minor mishap, the *Bannockburn* was considered to be a sturdy and reliable vessel. Owned by the Montreal Transportation Company, the steamer's typical journey would see her carry various cargoes on the upward trip, while transporting grain on her return.

On November 20, 1902, the *Bannockburn* had completed loading 85,000 bushels of grain at Port Arthur, Ontario. The crew latched down the cargo hatches tightly knowing weather on Lake Superior in November to be treacherous. Everyone on board was in good spirits since the shipping season was to close in a few weeks.

Even the *Bannockburn*'s master, Captain James McMaugh, was overly anxious to start the voyage and while steering the vessel away from the Port Arthur grain elevators, he inadvertently grounded her before the ship had even left the harbor. A quick check by the crew revealed no damage, but much of the *Bannockburn*'s hold space was full of grain and this limited the crew's inspection. With the *Bannockburn* seemly undamaged, Captain McMaugh was able to free his vessel the next day and she continued her journey out into Lake Superior.

Good progress was initially made, but soon the wind picked up in velocity and visibility was reduced. Captain McMaugh had enough experience that he probably recognized that a storm was going to descend and by evening it arrived, unleashing its fury over Lake Superior.

Although it was considered to be one of the fiercest storms of the season, all the steamers on the lake except the *Bannockburn* survived. When she became overdue at Sault Ste. Marie, everyone expected that she would eventually show up. It was suggested that the steamer was probably delayed after sheltering along the north shoreline, but more days passed and there was still no sighting of the Bannockburn. By November 27, her owners had officially written off the Bannockburn as lost. Rumors that she had gone aground along some isolated shoreline kept some hopes alive, but all searches failed to locate the vessel or any wreckage.

The fate of the *Bannockburn* remained a mystery until December 12, when a single life jacket bearing the steamer's name was discovered on the beach. Although this was the only wreckage recovered from the vessel it confirmed to those investigating that she had foundered that night during the storm, and the lack of wreckage or bodies also implied that the steamer sank rapidly. Since all other vessels had survived the storm, it was thought that the reason for the loss must have resulted from the earlier grounding. It seemed most likely that the vessel sustained some structural damage that weakened her to the extent that she foundered quickly in the fierce weather. The *Bannockburn*'s impatience to end the season led to her demise.

Owner: Montreal Transportation Company
Builder: Sir Raylton Dixon and Company
Dimensions: 245.0 x 40.1 x 18.4, 1,620 gt.
Built: 1893 at Middlebrough on Tees, England

Queen of the West

August 30, 1903
Lake Erie

On August 30, 1903, the wooden propeller *Queen of the West* departed Escanaba, Michigan, bound for Erie, Pennsylvania, with a cargo of iron ore. The weather was miserable, but to begin with the propeller made good progress in the heavy seas. However, by the time she reached Lake Erie, a leak was discovered in the aft section of the vessel. Water was rising in the holds, and the rate of flooding could only be slowed by keeping her traveling at full speed.

Salvation arrived in the shape of the steamer *Codorus,* which sighted the *Queen of the West* under distress and, while still at full speed, pulled alongside the strickeb ship to transfer her crewmen. All were saved except one man, who perished when he fell while trying to jump over to the *Codorus*'s deck. As the rescuing ship pulled away, the *Queen of the West* sank.

Owner: John Kelderhouse
Builder: William Crosthwaite
Dimensions: 215.0 x 32.5 x 16.2, 818 gt.
Built: 1881 at West Bay City, Michigan

Iosco and *Olive Jeanette*

September 1, 1905
Lake Superior

The *Iosco* left Superior Harbor with its tow—the schooner-barge *Olive Jeanette*—on Thursday, August 31, 1905, bound for Cleveland with a cargo of iron ore. On September 1, a northeasterly gale roared across the lakes, causing every vessel on Lake Superior to seek shelter at the nearest port. Throughout the day, several ports reported winds in excess of 50 mph and the lighthouse at the upper portage entry pier was toppled by waves whipped to mountainous size by the wind.

As the gale continued to roll across Lake Superior on September 2, the steamer *Martin Mullen*, east of the Huron Islands, sighted the *Iosco* and *Olive Jeanette*. The master of the *Mullen* later stated that each vessel seemed to be handling the gale. Unbeknown to him, this would be the last sighting of the two ships. The *Iosco* and *Olive Jeanette* foundered that night with all hands.

Although there were no survivors, there was a large amount of wreckage, and we can speculate to what happened that night. With its seams leaking, the *Iosco* cut loose the towline from the *Olive Jeanette* and sought the closest shelter—Keweenaw Bay. But, as each wave battered the *Iosco*, her holds filled with water and she began to settle lower. Eventually, some of the hatch covers broke free, and she slipped under the waves. The crew abandoned to the ship's yawl, which headed toward land but was overturned as it reached the breakers near the shoreline. The crew that survived and reached shore succumbed to hypothermia or shock.

The *Olive Jeanette* dropped her anchors and tried to ride out the gale. Like the *Iosco*, her holds were also slowly filling with water. Realizing that she would not survive the night, her master tried to set some canvas in an attempt to reach shore, but the sails tore away, leaving his ship helpless. Without power, the *Olive Jeanette* fell into the trough of the waves and sank beneath them. The crew then lashed themselves to the masts and spars in hopes of rescue, but the waves toppled them into the water. All of the 26 crewmen aboard the *Iosco* and *Olive Jeanette* were lost.

RIGHT: The steamer *Bannockburn* foundered on Lake Superior in 1902. The *Bannockburn*'s dimensions were designed so the vessel could traverse the Welland Canal. (See page 40)

BELOW RIGHT: A small passenger and package freight steamer that had recently left Collingwood, Ontario, and sailed out onto Lake Huron, the wooden propeller *Northern Belle* burned in Byng Inlet, Georgian Bay, on November 6, 1898. The stern section of the vessel was engulfed by the flames first and the fire spread quickly through the vessel. All on board were able to escape safely, but the *Northern Belle* burned to the waterline and was declared a total loss.

Iosco
Owner: W. A. Hawgood and Company
Builder: F. W.Wheeler
Dimensions: 291.0 x 41.0 x 18.8, 2,051 gt.
Built: 1891 at West Bay City, Michigan

Olive Jeanette
Owner: W. A. Hawgood and Company
Builder: F. W. Wheeler and Company
Dimensions: 242.0 x 39.0 x 16.0, 1,271 gt.
Built: 1890 at West Bay City, Michigan

RIGHT: The steamer *Iosco* vanished on Lake Superior in 1905. The *Iosco* was a near identical vessel to the steamer *L. R. Doty*.

BELOW AND BOTTOM RIGHT: The schooner barge *Olive Jeanette* was being towed by the *L.R. Doty* during a fall gale in 1898 when a storm arose. The *Doty* foundered, but the *Olive Jeanette* survived the gale (see page 42). Seven years later she disappeared along with the steamer *Iosco* on Lake Superior.

Sevona

September 2, 1905
Lake Superior

The early morning of September 2, 1905 saw the steel steamer *Sevona* attempting to seek shelter behind the Apostle Islands from a severe Lake Superior storm. Instead of finding a safe haven, however, she crashed against Sand Island Reef and immediately broke in two. With the waves pounding against the disintegrating steamer, her crew had to abandon ship. Sixteen in the stern escaped into the two lifeboats, but the remaining seven crewmen in the forward section had none, and resorted to using hatch covers to make for shore. While those lucky enough to have a place in the boats survived, the men on hatch covers could not withstand the strength of the surf and all were drowned.

Owner: John Mitchell
Builder: F. W. Wheeler and Company
Dimensions: 372.5 x 41.0 x 24.6, 3,166 gt.
Built: 1890 at West Bay City, Michigan

Pretoria

September 2, 1905
Lake Superior

The schooner barge *Pretoria* is best known as one of the largest wooden vessels to serve on the Great Lakes. On September 2, 1905, the steamer *Venezuela* was towing her from Two Harbors, Minnesota. Both vessels were fully laden with iron ore. That night, the two ships were caught in a violent fall gale and headed for the nearby shelter of the Apostle Islands. Before they reached safety, however, the steering gear aboard the *Pretoria* failed and the towline broke. The *Venezuela* searched for the schooner-barge, but could not find her in the darkness and mountainous seas. The powerless *Pretoria* was adrift with waves washing over her decks and water penetrating her holds. It was clear to all on board that it was all over for the schooner-barge, and her crew rushed for the lifeboat as she started to sink. They were able to launch it in time, but the lifeboat capsized while approaching the shore, and the heavy surf quickly drowned five of the crewmen: those remaining were able to hold onto the boat until it floated ashore.

Owner: James Davidson
Builder: Captain James Davidson
Dimensions: 338.4 x 44.0 x 23.0, 2,790 gt.
Built: 1900 at West Bay City, Michigan

Minnedosa

October 20, 1905
Lake Huron

Launched in 1890, the *Minnedosa* was the largest schooner ever built in Canada. Capable of reaching speeds of 15 knots (nearly 17 mph), she was as fast as any steamer of the day. On October 20, 1905, under the tow of the steamer *Westmount*, she was caught in a severe fall gale on Lake Huron. The two vessels were attempting to reach the safety of Harbor Beach when the *Minnedosa* vanished from sight. The schooner had suddenly foundered, taking all eight crewmen down with her. The most likely explanation for the tragedy is that her seams had worked free during the gale and the ship had subsequently became waterlogged.

Owner: Montreal Transportation Company
Builder: Henry Rooney
Dimensions: 245.0 x 36.3 x 15.1, 1,315 gt.
Built: 1890 at Kingston, Ontario

ABOVE: The steamer *Sevona* broke in two during a fall gale on Lake Superior in 1905. (See page 44)

Frank Rockefeller

November 2, 1905
Lake Superior

See *Meteor*, November 21, 1969 (page 133).

Monkshaven

November 27, 1905
Lake Superior

In a severe Lake Superior gale, the steel turret steamer *Monkshaven* grounded off Angus Island, on November 27, 1905, while endeavoring to make the shelter of Thunder Bay. The bow of the steamer was driven nearly out of the water, allowing all the crew to reach shore with ease. *Monkshaven* was severely damaged and declared a total loss; however, salvagers were able to pull her off the following year.

Owner: Algoma Central Line
Builder: J. Readhead and Co.
Dimensions: 249.0 x 36.0 x 18.0, 1425 gt.
Built: 1882

Madeira

November 28, 1905
Lake Superior

Madeira's wheel seen
with divers Dick Metz, Ed
Langlois, Bruce Keeley, and
Vince Jordan.

On November 28, 1905, the steel barge *Madeira,*
which had been under the tow of the steamer *William
Edenborn,* stranded near Split Rock Point, Lake
Superior. The two vessels had been struggling in a
severe gale, and when the *Edenborn*'s hatch covers
began to fail, the steamer let go the towline. Without
power, the barge drifted ashore at the base of a cliff,
which one heroic crewman was able to climb with a
rope, allowing five others to follow. One man, however, was swept overboard and lost. The *Madeira* was
pounded to pieces on the rocks.

Owner: Pittsburgh Steamship Company
Builder: Chicago Shipbuilding Company
Dimensions: 436.0 x 50.2 x 24.2, 5,039 gt.
Built: 1900 at Chicago, Illinois

Mataafa

November 28/29, 1905
Lake Superior

November storms on Lake Superior have no equal. With mountainous seas, sub-zero temperatures, blinding snow, and hurricane-strength winds, these storms have caused the greatest
destruction and tragedy among sailors of the Great Lakes. The last days of November 1905
were particularly wicked. On November 26, Lake Superior was relatively calm. The previous
week had unleashed a severe snowstorm keeping vessels in port, so a break in the weather was
a welcome relief. Dozens of vessels steamed out into the lake, hoping to make one more trip
before the end of the season.

On the morning of November 27, the weather forecast told of cold and fair conditions. At
Duluth, Minnesota, the steamer *Mataafa* was preparing to set sail with its consort barge *James
Nasmyth.* In command of the *Mataafa* was Captain R. F. Humble. Captain Humble had spent
16 years sailing on the Great Lakes, and had great confidence in his vessel.

At 3:30 pm, the *Mataafa* cleared the Duluth harbor piers with her barge. Both vessels were
fully laden with iron ore destined for the steel plants along Lake Erie. The weather had
worsened—winds began to gust with some snow flurries—and Captain Humble had some
reservations, but the *Mataafa* was a young staunch steamer that had already weathered many
storms through its six years in service.

The *Mataafa* and the *Nasmyth* made good progress, but the weather conditions continued
to deteriorate. The gusts of wind and snow turned into a raging blizzard. Waves crashed over
the spar deck and swirled down the length of the vessel. Captain Humble began to have great
concern for his vessel.

By 7:30 pm, the two vessels were off Two Harbors, Minnesota, when the storm's full force
struck. Massive waves crashed over the pilothouse and the already limited visibility dropped
down to nearly nothing. Crewmen down below struggled to stay on their feet. Firemen
continued to shovel coal into the boilers, while the chief engineer throttled the engine as the
screw was lifted and fell back into the rolling waves.

ABOVE LEFT: The *Minnedosa* was the largest schooner built in Canada to sail on the Great Lakes. It would disappear in 1905 on Lake Huron.

BELOW LEFT: The *Monkshaven* crashed onto a reef on Lake Superior during a severe fall storm in 1905. The steamer was pulled off the reef, but sank while proceeding to the ship breakers.

ABOVE: The steel steamer *Mataafa* was launched as the *Pennsylvania* in 1899 at Lorain, Ohio.

On the morning of November 28, the *Mataafa* was still being punished by the storm. Although the vessel had been steaming for over ten hours, she and *Nasmyth* had made little headway, so Captain Humble passed the order to turn back to shelter of Duluth. This required the *Mataafa* to fall into the trough of the waves, then swing her bow around. After successfully completing this dangerous maneuver, the two vessels headed towards Duluth.

Over the next several hours, they inched their way along the north shore. After noon, Captain Humble was able to see the shoreline as the snowfall let up. As the *Mataafa* caught sight of Duluth, he caught sight of two vessels entering the harbor. They were the steamer *R. W. England* and the steamer *Isaac L. Ellwood*.

The *R. W. England* was approaching the Duluth Ship Canal when her master realized that she was not going to make the piers. The steamer attempted to turn back into Lake Superior, but the giant waves pushed her ashore. The *R. W. England* eventually ended up high on the beach, and although the crew was safe, the vessel had suffered severe damage.

The *Isaac L. Ellwood* also attempted to enter the ship canal. She had spent several hours anchored in the open waiting for better weather and had begun to take on water in the hold. Her master had no choice but head for shelter before his vessel foundered under him. The *Ellwood* reached the canal by 1:00 pm and headed directly through the two piers. However, a large wave sent her crashing into the north pier, tearing plates in her hull. The *Ellwood* then bounced off the pier into the south pier, causing still more damage to her hull, before making the harbor. Spectators cheered as she was pulled into the shallow waters by tugs. The *Isaac L. Ellwood* quickly settled to the bottom, but her crew was safe.

The *Mataafa* and *Nasmyth* reached the entrance to the ship canal at 2:15 pm, but the dreadful conditions prevented bringing the consort *Nasmyth* through the narrow ship canal. Captain Humble ordered the towline dropped a few miles before the harbor entry piers. The barge then dropped its anchors. Fortunately they held, and the *Nasmyth* was able to ride out the storm. Captain Humble then ordered the *Mataafa* at full steam ahead toward the entry piers. Just as the steamer approached them, a giant wave lifted *Mataafa* so high that her bow stuck bottom. The blow sent the vessel's stern careening into the north pier. Another wave forced her to turn at right angles to the pier. Although the steamer still had full power, it seemed to be immobilized, and Captain Humble realized that her rudder had been sheared off when the vessel struck. The *Mataafa* was now disabled and at the mercy of the storm. Wave after wave pushed the steamer against the concrete pier until another large wave pushed her outside the pier into nearby shallow water. Captain Humble's gamble of entering the ship canal had gone disastrously wrong.

After the *Mataafa* struck hard aground, it began to break in two. The stern section began to settle lower in the water, allowing waves to wash over the sinking stern extinguishing the boilers and the only source of heat and power on the vessel. With the temperature nearly -13°C and the stern breaking apart, the crewmen aft were in desperate shape. The second mate, who had been sent aft to help release the towline earlier, decided to risk crossing the open deck to the forward section. Along with three other crewmen, the men made their way along the railing. Icy waves crashed over them nearly breaking their grasp of the thin wire, but three men reached forward. One crewman, after nearly being washed overboard several times, elected to join the eight other crewmen on the stern section. These men had little protection from the elements, seeking refuge under the smokestack as the winds peaked at over 60 mph.

The remaining 15 crewmen took refuge in the forepeak. Conditions were little better than at the stern, as water careened through broken portholes and through broken doors. The men had only the heat from a few lamps. There was no food or drink, so some broke off icicles and sucked on them. Captain Humble ordered the men to stay on their feet, even though they were all exhausted from the ordeal.

However, there was some hope for the crew of the *Mataafa*. They could see bonfires blazing through the snowstorm from along the shore where nearly 40,000 people from Duluth had gathered along the piers and beaches keeping a vigil. The Coast Guard had attempted to get a line aboard and rig a breeches buoy, but the line quickly froze and broke. No lifeboats or any other attempts would be made while the tempest still raged on Lake Superior.

The morning of November 29 brought better weather. The wind and seas had decreased, allowing the Coast Guard to launch their boat out to the *Mataafa*. Captain Humble and the other crewmen forward were quickly taken off. Before Captain Humble left his steamer, he ventured back to the stern. There he sighted several crewmen frozen to death. Their bodies were encased by ice and had to be chopped free to be taken off the vessel. In all, nine crewmen in the stern section died of exposure or were washed overboard. That day also the barge *James Nasmyth* was towed into port. Although it was battered, the vessel and crew survived the storm.

The *Mataafa* had been broken in two and was severely damaged; in spite of this, the steamer was recovered some six months later. In 1906, she was rebuilt at a cost of nearly $100,000, but resumed a long career on the Great Lakes.

In 1958, the Nicholson Transit Company purchased the *Mataafa*, fitting out the 60-year-old steamer into service as an automobile carrier. Capable of carrying 500 vehicles from Detroit to Buffalo, the *Mataafa* exchanged hands several times before being purchased by Marine Salvage Ltd. in 1965. That same year, *Mataafa* passed down the Welland Canal under her own power for the last time. On July 19, 1965, the *Mataafa* arrived at Hamburg, Germany, to be scrapped.

Even though the tragedy of that late November storm of 1905 had affected all of Lake Superior, it has been known ever since as the "*Mataafa* Storm."

Owner: Minnesota Steamship Company
Builder: Cleveland Shipbuilding Company
Dimensions: 429.6 x 50.0 x 25.0, 4,840 gt.
Built: 1899 at Lorain, Ohio

Ira H. Owen

November 28/29, 1905
Lake Superior

The *Ira H. Owen* was blowing distress signals and in near sinking condition when spotted by another steamer, the *H. R. Nye,* off the Apostle Islands during the night of November 28, 1905. Unhappily for the *Owen*, the *Nye* could not offer aid, since she was barely staying afloat herself

RIGHT: The steamer *Mataafa* being pounded by huge waves while stranded off Duluth, Minnesota, in 1905.

BELOW RIGHT: A view of the *Mataafa* after the storm. Notice the large breaks amidships in the hull.

BOTTOM RIGHT: A view of the *Mataafa*'s stern after the 1905 storm. Nine men perished on the aft section near the smokestack.

in the fierce winds howling across Lake Superior. This was the last time the *Owen* would be seen in one piece. Later, the steamer *Sir William Siemens* recovered wreckage near the same location, including life preservers marked "S.S. *Ira H. Owen*." The number of lives preserved that night, however, amounted to none—all 19 of the *Owen*'s crew perished.

Owner: Owen Transportation Company
Builder: Globe Iron Works Company
Dimensions: 262.0 x 39.0 x 19.0, 1,753 gt.
Built: 1887 at Cleveland, Ohio

RIGHT: The steel steamer *Lafayette* would run ashore in a gale on Lake Superior in 1905.

BELOW RIGHT: The *Ira H. Owen* shown going through the locks at the "Soo." Notice the steamer has two smokestacks unusually placed side-by-side.

Lafayette

November 29, 1905
Lake Superior

The steel propeller *Lafayette* was driven against the cliffs of Encampment Island, off Two Harbors, Ontario, during a strong northeasterly gale. During the storm her tow, the *Manila,* had rammed her, leaving *Lafayette* at the mercy of the waves. Only one life was lost, despite *Lafayette* breaking in two, and 25 crewmen were saved. The cost of the loss of cargo and the vessel herself were calculated to be $400,000. Later, the engines of the five-year-old ship were salvaged, and by 1909 were driving the new steamer *J. S. Ashley*.

Owner: W. A. Hawgood
Builder: American Shipbuilding Company
Dimensions: 454.0 x 50 x 28.5, 5,113 gt.
Built: 1900 at Lorain, Ohio

Armenia

May 9, 1906
Lake Erie

The schooner-barge *Armenia,* under the tow of steamer *Fred Pabst,* foundered near Pelee Island Light on Lake Erie, the ships having been caught in an unusually strong spring gale. The *Armenia*'s old hull could not withstand the storm and began to take on water fast. She signaled the *Pabst* that she needed assistance, and the steamer dropped the towline and headed for her. Just as the men of the *Armenia* were pulled aboard, she plunged to the bottom of the lake. Coincidentally, *Armenia*'s sister ship, the *Algeria,* had also sunk at nearby Cleveland harbor breakwater six days earlier. *Algeria*'s crew was not so lucky, and two lives were lost.

Owner: West Division Steamship Company
Builder: James Davidson
Dimensions: 288.6 x 44.6 x 24.0, 2,040 gt.
Built: 1896 at West Bay City, Michigan

M. I. Wilcox

May 10, 1906
Lake Erie

Sailors are superstitious about the vessels on which they brave the waters. If the ship has operated without incident, they will spend the whole shipping season aboard, but if she has a reputation for being accident-prone, they will leave as soon as she ties up. Most considered the schooner-barge *M. I. Wilcox* to be a "jinxed" vessel—she had had over 15 large repairs and five major accidents. Crewmen who had served aboard her said that the cranky *Wilcox* leaked easily and often. Her steam pumps were also known to fail, and required round the clock attention. Blame for her loss was to fall on these faulty pumps after the *Wilcox* foundered off Colchester, Ontario, during a spring gale. The crewman in charge of watching them had been distracted, and by the time he checked them the vessel was nearly waterlogged. All four crew abandoned ship and were rescued a short time later, but the *M. I. Wilcox* was a total loss.

Owner: Captain Summerville
Builder: Bailey Brothers
Dimensions: 137.0 x 27.5 x 12.7, 377 gt.
Built: 1868 at Toledo, Ohio

Monarch

December 6, 1906
Lake Superior

On December 6, 1906, the wooden package steamer *Monarch* left Port Arthur, Ontario, on her last trip of the season. On watch was the master, Captain Edward Robertson. The captain was attempting to set course from Thunder Bay around Isle Royale, but this task was unusually difficult since visibility was reduced to mere feet by worsening weather conditions. Wind and waves were becoming ever more violent, and water rushed over the decks. With snow also hampering visibility there was little choice for Captain Robertson but to steer by instinct alone.

Unable to set his bearings properly, the *Monarch* soon veered off course. Disaster was inevitable—she struck head-on into Blake's Point, Isle Royale, her bow ending up only 25 feet from the shore, while the stern was still unsupported in deep water. Robertson issued an order to keep the engine running, hoping to keep the ship from slipping off the rocks, but the chief engineer reported water pouring into the engine room through the punctured hull. The situation was desperate and everyone onboard knew it was only a matter of time before the *Monarch*'s demise.

Captain Robertson ordered the lifeboat lowered to run a line ashore, but it was smashed before it could be landed and so a decision was made to drop a crewman over the side with a rope attached. He would be swung until he could reach a nearby rock outcropping. A deckhand, J. D. McCullum, was selected for the perilous task and he was duly lowered over the side of the vessel with a line tied around his waist. Two times he was swung over the outcropping, but could not hold on. On the third attempt he was swung out, but the rope broke. Luckily, McCullum landed on the rock and was able to hold on. Another line was thrown over to him and he climbed up the high cliffs to secure it to a tree. One by one, the remaining crewmen and passengers used the rope to cross over the lake. Shortly after the last man reached safety, the *Monarch*'s bow rose out of the water while the stern broke off and sank.

The survivors quickly built a fire from driftwood to keep warm, but without shelter or food, they could not hope to last long. Unknown to them, however, the Passage Island light keeper had spotted the fire, but was powerless to take action until the storm abated. It was

wreck of the Monarch

December 9, by the time that the light keeper was able to row over to the *Monarch* survivors. He returned to the lighthouse with the ship's purser and, soon after, they had flagged down an outbound steamer. A few hours later, the tug *James Whalen* headed out from Port Arthur for the remainder of the survivors. All of the exhausted crew and passengers were brought onboard suffering from frostbite and exposure, although all were fortunate enough to eventually recover from their ordeal. Following the disaster, Deckhand McCullum was awarded a medal from the Royal Humane Society for his bravery in the rescue of passengers and fellow crewmen.

Owner: Northern Navigation Company
Builder: Dyble Shipyard
Dimensions: 242.0 x 35.0 x 14.8, 2,017 gt.
Built: 1888 at Sarnia, Ontario

ABOVE: The passenger steamer *Monarch* at Isle Royale in 1906. She lost her way before crashing ashore on Lake Superior during a blizzard.

BELOW LEFT: The *Queen of the Lakes* seen at winter lay up. On November 28, 1906, the schooner *Queen of the Lakes* was bound for Kingston, Ontario, when caught in a fall gale on Lake Ontario. The wind and waves crashed over the schooner's deck and the strain caused her hull to leak. Even with bilge pumps working flat out, water rose higher and higher in the hold. Then the waterlogged *Queen of the Lakes* began to list. Her crew hastily launched the lifeboat and pulled away just as the schooner capsized and sank.

Cyprus

October 11, 1907
Lake Superior

The lifespan of steamers on the Great Lakes varies considerably. At one end of the spectrum is the steamer *John R. Emery,* which was launched in 1905 and was still in operation in 1998, 93 years later. At the other end, however, is the steamer *Cyprus*.

The *Cyprus* left Superior, Wisconsin, on the morning of October 9, 1907, with a cargo of iron ore. The weather worsened, and waves began to roll over the decks, spilling into *Cyprus*'s hold. The master ordered the pumps to be started, and water mixed with ore was pumped out, turning the ship's wake a rusty-brown. Just off Deer Park, Michigan, the ship suddenly lurched over and sank. It was later discovered that the water had destabilized the cargo: as the *Cyprus* had rolled in the waves, so the cargo shifted, capsizing the steamer. Only one man reached shore alive, 22 others perishing on a vessel with one of the shortest life spans of any on the Great Lakes. Launched September 17, 1907, she had remained in operation for only 24 days!

Owner: Lackawanna Steamship Company
Builder: American Shipbuilding
Dimensions: 420.0 x 52.0 x 28.0, 4,900 gt.
Built: 1907 at Lorain, Ohio

Neshoto

September 27, 1908
Lake Superior

The wooden steamer *Neshoto*, out from Superior, Wisconsin, and bound for Buffalo with a load of iron ore, veered off course on September 27, 1908. On land, a forest fire had started and was raging. Smoke masked the lakeshore and in these conditions of poor visibility, the vessel lost her way and plowed into the shallow banks off Crisp Point, Lake Superior. The crew of the *Neshoto* tried to free her, but she was firmly aground, though not badly damaged. However, before any additional assistance could be requested, the wind increased and the crew watched helplessly from the shore as the steamer was pulverized in the surf. She was declared a total loss.

Owner: J. C. Gilchrist Company
Builder: Quayle and Son
Dimensions: 284.0 x 43.0 x 22.0
Built: 1889 at Cleveland, Ohio

Lizzie A. Law

November 8, 1908
Lake Superior

The schooner-barges *Selden Marvin* and *Lizzie A. Law* were under the tow of the steamer *Edward Hines*, headed for Duluth with their holds filled with coal. Like most schooner-barges, the *Lizzie A. Law* had been launched as a schooner for the grain trade, but competition from faster and larger steamers saw her topmast removed, and she became one of many tow barges on the lakes. On November 8, 1908, as the ships passed the Keweenaw Peninsula, they were caught in a severe gale, which broke the towlines, leaving both barges on their own to reach

safety. The gale's ferocity proved too much for the *Lizzie A. Law*, which grounded on a sand-bar off Huron Island. All seven crew reached shore, but the waves pounded the ship to pieces.

Owner: Hines Lumber Company
Builder: Fitzgerald Dry Dock
Dimensions: 196.1 x 33.9 x 13.9, 747 gt.
Built: June 1875 at Port Huron, Michigan

D. M. Clemson

December 1, 1908
Lake Superior

The steel steamer *D. M. Clemson* departed Lorain, Ohio, on November 28, 1908, fully laden with coal. By November 30, she had locked through the "Soo" and was headed out onto Lake Superior. The next day a gale struck and the vessel encountered 20-foot waves along with sub zero temperatures. Wave after wave must have crashed over her decks; hatch covers being washed away and the vessel slowly settling lower in the water.

One of the largest vessels afloat, the *Clemson* was considered staunch, having survived the 1905 storm even after losing her hatch covers and becoming badly waterlogged. So when she was reported overdue at Duluth, her owners thought she must have taken the longer northern route or sought shelter in some isolated section of Lake Superior. After a few more days, how-ever, they became more concerned and asked for a search to be made for their missing ship. Tugs were dispatched from Port Arthur and cruised along the shoreline hoping to find the *D. M. Clemson* stranded or disabled.

On December 6, wreckage from ship was discovered along the shoreline near Whitefish Point. Several lifesaving stations recovered hatch covers along with a water barrel with "D. M. Clemson" painted on one end. When additional wreckage was discovered, the lifesaving stations stayed in operation for several more days to continue with the search. But it became increasingly clear that the *Clemson* had foundered during the gale taking all the crew onboard. The search only recovered one body, however, and the beach patrols were ended on December 22.

The loss of the vessel remained a mystery, but some clues were uncovered. The *Clemson* had grounded earlier in the month with damage to some of the hull plates, and after tempo-rary repairs had been made, she continued in operation, being scheduled for repairs after her winter lay up. Other clues to the loss were provided by several vessels that had survived the gale. Many arrived in port heavily coated in thick ice, reducing the available freeboard.

It was decided that the loss of the *D. M. Clemson* was most likely caused by the loss of freeboard from water flooding her hold after the loss of her hatches. With the additional bur-den of ice forming along the deck, she sank with all hands.

Owner: A. B. Wolvin
Builder: Superior Shipbuilding Company
Dimensions: 468.0 x 52.0 x 28.0, 5,531 gt.
Built: 1903 at West Superior, Wisconsin

Adella Shores

April 29, 1909
Lake Superior

In 1894, the Shores Lumber Company received their newest vessel, the *Adella Shores*. After the hull was completed at Gibraltar, Michigan, the company had the vessel brought to their

lumber mills at Ashland, Wisconsin. There the vessel was formally launched with great fanfare, though, unlike other launchings, the *Adella Shores* was christened with a bottle of water instead of alcohol.

The ship quickly proved to be dependable. She usually carried lumber cargoes down to the lower lakes and bulk cargoes on the return trips. As the *Adella Shores'* deck was, time after time, piled high with freshly cut lumber, the great forests that once stood along the shores of the Great Lakes were depleted.

Only four years after her launch, however, the Shores Lumber Company sold the vessel to another lumber firm. A few years later she was sold again—to Manx Transportation Company in 1908. During this time the steamer continued in the lumber trade.

The *Adella Shores* started the 1909 season under new ownership and by late April 1909 the steamer left Ludington with a load of salt bound for Duluth. The steamer's master, Captain Holmes, steered her up Lake Michigan without incident and on April 29 the *Shores* locked through the Sault Ste. Marie and headed into Lake Superior. A few hours later a fierce gale was directly over the steamer. Captain Holmes was undoubtedly concerned over his aged steamer, but though wind and waves were battering the vessel, he was probably more worried about ice. Even in April, there were large ice packs on the lake that could easily puncture a hull.

When the storm blew itself out, there was no sign of the *Adella Shores* on Lake Superior. Several vessels had spotted her leaving Whitefish Bay, but they lost sight of the ship during the gale. After the steamer had been overdue at Duluth for a week, all hope was given up for the ship and her 14 crewmen, and, eventually, reports of wreckage near Sable Point confirmed her destruction. No bodies were recovered from the *Shores*, but a crewman's coat was discovered on a crude raft created from the vessel's deck. Clearly, the crew of the *Adella Shores* had had time to abandon the vessel, but all must have perished soon after.

Owner: Shores Lumber Company
Builder: Wolverine Boat Company
Dimensions: 213.1 x 35.2 x 13.6, 776 gt.
Built: 1894 at Gibraltar, Michigan

Marquette & Bessemer No. 2

December 8, 1909
Lake Erie

Although storm warnings had been posted, the car ferry *Marquette & Bessemer No. 2* steamed out of Conneaut, Ohio, on the evening of December 8, 1909, and headed into Lake Erie aiming for Port Stanley, Ontario. During the night, the storm unleashed 70 mph winds, and snow squalls meant that visibility dropped to near zero. The valiant *No. 2* nevertheless reached her destination, battling through the mountainous waves. However, the weather made entering the harbor impossible, and the ship was forced to turn back into the storm and head for harbor at Rondeau, Ontario, instead. But shelter was not to be found at Rondeau either; conditions there again prevented the ferry from entering harbor. Finally, the *No. 2* headed back to Conneaut, crossing Lake Erie a second time, only to find that this harbor, too, was impossible to enter in the storm.

After steaming all night, the *Marquette & Bessemer No.2* had exhausted its coal supply and fell into the trough of the waves, foundering with all 19 hands.

Owner: Marquette and Bessemer Dock Navigation Company
Builder: American Shipbuilding Company
Dimensions: 338.0 x 54.0 x 19.5, 2,514 gt.
Built: 1905 at Cleveland, Ohio

RIGHT: The steamer *D. M. Clemson* vanished on Lake Superior in 1908. None of the bodies of the 24 men on board were ever found. (See page 58)

BELOW RIGHT: The lumber hooker *Adella Shores* vanished on Lake Superior in 1909—it is believed between Munising, Michigan, and Whitefish Bay. She is seen here with a typical full load of lumber, although when she was lost her cargo was salt. (See page 58)

BOTTOM RIGHT: The iron steamer *Clarion* was launched in 1881 to serve the Anchor Line between Chicago, Milwaukee, Buffalo, and Erie, Pennsylvania. On December 8, 1909, she had entered Lake Erie and was heading east toward Buffalo and Erie on her last trip of the season when she suddenly erupted in flames off Pelee Island. The crew tried in vain to extinguish the inferno, but it was clear that the vessel was burning out of control. The master, along with 11 crewmen, abandoned ship in the steel lifeboat, which drifted away from the steamer, never to be seen again. The remaining seven crewmen attempted to escape using the steamer's wooden yawl, but it capsized, spilling all aboard into the water. Six swam back and held onto the remains of the *Clarion* from where they were rescued by a passing steamer.

Ann Arbor No. 1

May 8, 1910
Lake Michigan

The first car ferry designed for the Great Lakes was launched in 1892 as the *Ann Arbor No. 1*. Her wooden hull could easily carry 24 railcars across Lake Michigan from Frankfort to various other ports the railroad served, and for many years she made the crossing without incident. But on May 8, 1910, the *Ann Arbor No. 1* caught fire at her dock at Manitowoc while loading 20 railcars of lumber. Her aged timbers easily ignited, and soon the whole vessel was ablaze from stem to stern. Attempts to extinguish the fire were futile, and the car ferry burned to the waterline. Her remains were later towed out and scuttled nearby.

Two conflicting explanations for the cause of the blaze circulated. The chief engineer stated that he saw a young deckhand with a flaming torch as shouts of fire rang out, while others averred that combusting machinery started the blaze.

Owner: Ann Arbor and Northern Michigan Railroad
Builder: Craig Shipbuilding Company
Dimensions: 260.4 x 53.0 x 14.7, 1,127 gt.
Built: 1892 at Toledo, Ohio

ABOVE: The car ferry *Marquette & Bessemer No. 2* could not safely enter a harbor during a fall storm on Lake Erie in 1909, and foundered. Her exact location is still not known. (See page 60)

Zenith City

July 26, 1910
Lake Huron

On July 26, 1910, the steel steamer *Zenith City,* one of the first two vessels on the lakes to measure over 400 feet, departed Marquette with a cargo of iron ore. Visibility was poor due to fog, but a safe course was set passing north of Au Sable Point. However, the wheelsman strayed from the compass bearing and the steamer veered off course. Still in heavy fog, the *Zenith City* struck Au Sable Reef at full speed. She was heavily loaded, and attempts to free her failed. However, the lake was calm and there was no danger of the her sinking. Eventually a salvage team was able to free the stranded vessel.

ABOVE: The 459-foot steel steamer *Zenith City* was wrecked on Au Sable Reef, Lake Superior, in 1910. This photograph shows the Zenith proceeding light—in other words without cargo.

Owner: *Zenith City* Transportation Company
Builder: Chicago Shipbuilding Company
Dimensions: 459.0 x 48.3 x 23.3, 3,850 gt.
Built: 1895 at Chicago, Illinois

Pere Marquette No. 18

September 9, 1910
Lake Michigan

On September 9, 1910, the steel passenger and car ferry *Pere Marquette No. 18* was the first vessel on the Great Lakes to use a wireless to send an "SOS." The ferry was sailing across Lake Michigan when a crewman during his routine rounds discovered a leak under the crew's quarters. He alerted the master, who ordered every available crewman to discover the exact location of the leak. The master also ordered the bilge pumps started in the hope that the *Pere Marquette No. 18* could reach port before sinking, but the water rose higher and higher in the engine room, and with the ship settling deeper into the water, the crew was forced to jettison 12 railcars in an attempt to keep the vessel afloat. Just before the water extinguished the boilers, the master had the radioman send out an "SOS." A sister ship, the *Pere Marquette No. 17*, received the distress call and steamed to her aid. Just as she arrived on scene, *Pere Marquette No. 18* lurched over and foundered, drowning 29 of the 62 passengers and crew.

Owner: Pere Marquette Steamship Company
Builder: American Shipbuilding Company
Dimensions: 358.0 x 56.0 x 19.5, 2909 gt.
Built: 1902 at Cleveland, Ohio

Gunilda

August 11, 1911
Lake Superior

The demise of the steam yacht *Gunilda* was caused by the miserliness of her owner, William L. Harkness, a man of immense wealth. He refused to pay 15 dollars for a pilot to safely guide

LEFT AND BELOW: *Ann Arbor No. 1* was the first car ferry built for the Great Lakes. Here, onlookers watch her burning at the docks at Manitowoc, Wisconsin, in 1910. (See page 62)

the vessel into Nipigon Bay, Lake Superior, with the result that the *Gunilda* went hard aground on McGarvey Shoal. Indeed, she struck so forcefully that her bow was completely out of the water. The yacht needed a tug to free her, and one was immediately dispatched to the scene. When it arrived, the salvagers wanted to attach additional scows as a safety precaution. William Harkness, however, again refused the added expense, and ordered them to pull his yacht from the shoal immediately. As the tug started to pull the yacht free, the *Gunilda* began to list to starboard. No one had closed the portholes, and water steadily poured in. The *Gunilda* slid off McGarvey Shoal and sank. There were no injuries except to Mr. Harkness's pride.

Owner: William L. Harkness
Builder: Ramage and Ferguson
Dimensions: 177.0 x N/A x N/A, 385 gt.
Built: 1897 at Leith, Scotland

Three Brothers

September 27, 1911
Lake Michigan

With the capacity to carry over 900,000 board feet, the wooden steamer *Three Brothers* was servicing the lumber trade when she sprang a leak during a storm on Lake Michigan. Her master ordered that the steamer head for land before she sank, and the ship was able to reach South Manitou Island where she was beached on the island's sandy shore. However, she was beyond repair and abandoned on the island. That winter, storms forced her off the beach and she quickly sank in the deep water nearby. Today, the *Three Brothers* is a favorite among scuba divers.

Owner: White Transportation Company
Builder: Milwaukee Shipyard Company
Dimensions: 162.0 x 31.4 x 11.8, 583 gt.
Built: 1888 at Milwaukee, Wisconsin

Azov

October 22, 1911
Lake Huron

Sometimes a shipwreck mystery develops from conflicting information as the confusion that surrounds the schooner *Azov* exemplifies. This vessel was unusual in that she was lost twice! Little is known about the ship other than that she was one of the many schooners of the late 1860s plying across the Great Lakes. The first report of her demise came in 1870 and states the *Azov* collided with the propeller *Bristol* and eventually sank on Lake Ontario. Her story does not end there, however: another report states that the *Azov* capsized and foundered near Port Aux Barques, Lake Huron, on October 22, 1911. Were there two schooners named *Azov* with nearly identical dimensions? Was the original *Azov* salvaged from the bottom of Lake Ontario? It is unlikely that anyone will ever be completely sure, so the *Azov* will remain an enigma.

Owner: Unknown
Builder: J. Simpson
Dimensions: 108.4 x 23.7 x 10.0, 195 gt.
Built: 1866 at Wellington Square, Ontario

RIGHT: The steel car ferry *Pere Marquette No. 18* was not equipped with a stern gate which could have prevented her loss on Lake Michigan in 1910. (See page 63)

BELOW RIGHT: Built in 1902 *Pere Marquette No. 18* had an eventful career. Here she is seen in 1904 stuck in ice off Manitowoc, Wisconsin.

BOTTOM RIGHT: The *Three Brothers* fell victim to a fall storm on Lake Michigan. The wooden steamer sank off South Manitou Island in 1911.

Rouse Simmons

November 22, 1912
Lake Michigan

The schooner *Rouse Simmons*, known as the "Christmas Tree Ship," sailed every November and December along Lake Michigan. Her owner and master, Herman Schuenemann, operated a successful business selling the trees to Chicago's big hotels and theaters, and the brisk trade required sailing through these inhospitable weeks, notorious for ferocious gales.

On November 22, 1912, the *Rouse Simmons* departed Thompson, Michigan, bound for Chicago. It was her last trip of the season and on board were about 50,000 trees—nearly double the schooner's capacity—as well as crew and passengers. So loaded was the ship that onlookers reported that the trees were stacked so high on deck that the sails had to be raised an additional ten feet to clear them. As the *Rouse Simmons* sailed south toward Chicago, a fall storm struck Lake Michigan. Lashed by winds and heavy seas, the overburdened schooner's seams opened up, and she began to sink. However, the distressed "Christmas Tree Ship" was sighted off Two Rivers, Wisconsin, and the lifesaving service was alerted to her plight. A powered lifeboat was launched, but rescuers could not find the *Rouse Simmons*. The schooner had foundered before they could reach her. All perished on board—19 passengers and crewmen including Captain Schuenemann. The following spring, fishermen reported finding trees in their nets.

Owner: Captain Herman Schuenemann
Builder: Allen McLelland and Company
Dimensions: 123.5 x 27.6 x 8.4, 205 gt.
Built: 1868 at Milwaukee, Wisconsin

L. C. Waldo

November 8, 1913
Lake Superior

One of the worst storms ever to rage across the Great Lakes lasted from November 8 to November 13, 1913. Known as the "Great Storm," it was unprecedented in strength and in damage inflicted on the inland shipping community. Twelve vessels totally disappeared and scores of others were destroyed. Over 251 men were killed.

The *L. C. Waldo* was the first vessel to succumb to the great storm. She left Two Harbors bound for Erie, Pennsylvania, with a cargo of iron ore, and proceeded down Lake Superior until west of Keweenaw Point. The storm came upon the ship without warning. A huge wave broke over her, smashing the pilothouse and washing away all navigation equipment except for auxiliary steering gear and a pocket compass. Using this, the *Waldo* sought shelter behind the Keweenaw Peninsula, but the storm pushed her far off course, and she ran hard aground on Manitou Island. The aft crew ran forward, seeking protection, and just as the last man reached the forward cabins, the *Waldo* broke in two, leaving the crew without clothes, provisions, or heat. The *Waldo*'s master converted a bathtub into a makeshift fireplace, which provided enough warmth until the entire crew were rescued two days later.

Owner: Roby Transportation Company
Builder: F. W. Wheeler
Dimensions: 451.0 x 48.0 x 28.0, 4466 gt.
Built: 1896 at West Bay City, Michigan

RIGHT: The schooner *Azov* shown under tow on the St. Clair River. (See page 66)

BELOW RIGHT: The schooner *Rouse Simmons* became known as the "Christmas Tree Ship" along the ports on Lake Michigan because of her winter cargo.

BELOW: *Rouse Simmons* (at right of picture) seen at Sheboygan, Wisconsin.

TOP AND ABOVE: Two views of the side-wheel steamer *Flora*, which caught fire and was destroyed in 1912.

LEFT: The *City of Kalamazoo*.

John A. McGean

November 8, 1913
Lake Huron

The steamer *John A. McGean* was last sighted on November 7, 1913, off Tawas Point heading on a direct course for De Tour. She then foundered sometime on November 8, with all 23 crewmen lost. Although there was little wreckage at the time, divers discovered her overturned hull in 1985 off Port Hope, Michigan. From inspection, it appears that she was struck by a massive wave and plunged to the bottom.

Owner: Hutchinson and Company
Builder: American Shipbuilding Company
Dimensions: 432.0 x 52.0 x 28.0, 5,100 gt.
Built: 1908 at Lorain, Ohio

Hydrus

November 8, 1913
Lake Huron

The steel steamer *Hydrus* tempted fate twice through the storm. She had battled her way through it on Lake Superior and finally reached the "Soo" on November 8. Her master commented that the weather had made the trip down difficult, but he didn't realize that the storm had not reached its height, and the *Hydrus* continued south to Lake Huron. She soon encountered the full rage of the storm, was overwhelmed, and foundered off Lexington, Michigan. All 28 crewmen perished.

Owner: Interlake Steamship Company
Builder: American Shipbuilding Company
Dimensions: 436.0 x 50.0 x 28.0, 4,713 gt.
Built: 1903 at Lorain, Ohio

Plymouth

November 8, 1913
Lake Michigan

Believing the storm had abated, the tug *James H. Martin* and her tow, the barge *Plymouth*, sailed out from shelter behind St. Martin Island. However, once they were out in the expanse of Lake Michigan, the storm increased in ferocity. To survive, the *Martin* dropped her towline to the *Plymouth* and headed back for shelter. Meanwhile, the *Plymouth* dropped its anchors to ride out the storm. That night, it became clear to the *Plymouth*'s crew that the vessel was going to sink. The barge hoisted distress signals and the crew lashed themselves to the masts. However, no help would arrive in time to save them. The vessel eventually attracted the attention of the lifesavers, but the seven crewmen aboard had already frozen to death.

Owner: Baker et al.
Builder: Ira Lafrinier
Dimensions: 213.1 x 35.2 x 13.6, 776 gt.
Built: 1854 at Cleveland, Ohio

ABOVE: The steamer *Leafield* foundered on Lake Superior during the great storm of 1913 taking all 18 crewmen with her.

Leafield

November 8, 1913
Lake Superior

Stranded on rocks at Angus Island near Pie Island, Thunder Bay, the storm later pushed the *Leafield* off the rocks and she sank with a cargo of steel rails and track fastenings. All 28 crew were lost. Including the cargo, the vessel was valued at $144,100.

Owner: Algoma Central Steamship Company
Builder: Strand Slipway Company
Dimensions: 249.0 x 35.2 x 16.6, 1,454 gt.
Built: 1892 at Sunderland, England

Howard M. Hanna

November 9, 1913
Lake Huron

The *Howard M. Hanna* entered Lake Huron in clear weather during the early morning of November 9. By noon the wind had increased and there were snow flurries; by the afternoon the steamer was gripped in a violent gale. Waves crashed over the ship, tearing doors loose, smashing windows, and carrying away part of the cabin. The *Hanna* was unable to maintain headway and dropped into the trough of the waves. Rolling heavily, she also faced another problem: the waves had pushed her far off course and she was dangerously close to Port Austin Reef. At ten o'clock in the evening, the *Hanna* slammed into the reef and broke in two. Her crew waited two days before the Port Austin lifesaving crew could rescue them all.

Owner: Hanna Transit Company
Builder: American Shipbuilding Company
Dimensions: 504.0 x 54.0 x 30.0, 6,204 gt.
Built: 1908 at Cleveland, Ohio

LEFT: Sightseers visiting the *Plymouth*. They most likely had to venture across the ice to reach the vessel. (See page 72)

ABOVE AND BELOW: The steamers *Hydrus* (*above*) and *John A. McGean* (*below*) were two of many steamers lost on Lake Huron during the great storm of 1913. (See page 72)

Henry B. Smith

November 9, 1913
Lake Superior

The staunch steamer *Henry B. Smith* left Marquette with a hold full of iron ore at five o'clock on the afternoon of November 9. Witnesses reported seeing the steamer struggling in the heavy seas and, before snow squalls blocked her from sight, noticed the *Smith* attempting to turn back to port. It is assumed that the vessel foundered later that night, and all hands were lost. One clue to why the ship went down can be found in the evidence given by several dockhands, all of whom stated that the *Smith* left port still securing her hatches. If the vessel's hatches were not properly secured, waves could easily have flooded the holds, causing the steamer to founder.

Owner: Acme Transit Company
Builder: American Shipbuilding Company
Dimensions: 545.0 x 55.0 x 31.0, 6,631 gt.
Built: 1906 at Lorain, Ohio

Isaac M. Scott

November 9, 1913
Lake Huron

The steamer *Isaac M. Scott* was a few miles behind the *John A. McGean* when she disappeared. The *Scott* had left Cleveland, Ohio, with a crew of 28 men and was sighted on November 9, in great difficulty. It is presumed that she foundered during the terrible storm. Unlike other vessels lost, not a single body from the *Isaac M. Scott*'s crew was recovered.

Owner: Hanna and Company
Builder: American Shipbuilding Company
Dimensions: 504.0 x 54.0 x 30.0, 6,372 gt.
Built: 1909 at Lorain, Ohio

James Carruthers

November 9, 1913
Lake Huron

Launched May 22, 1913, the new steel steamer *James Carruthers* was the largest Canadian vessel afloat and was only on her third voyage when caught on Lake Huron in the storm. Unprepared for the fury unleashed, the *Carruthers* foundered with all hands, except one lucky crewman, John Thompson. Thompson was the ship's fireman, but was not aboard when the steamer sank. When he read newspaper reports of his own demise, he took a train home and arrived just as his own wake was in progress. His father, shocked to see his alive son, sang out, "It would be just like you to come back to attend your own funeral and you can get right out of the house until this thing blows over!"

Owner: St. Lawrence and Chicago Steam Navigation Company
Builder: Collingwood Shipbuilding Company.
Dimensions: 550.0 x 58.2 x 26.7, 7,862 gt.
Built: 1913 at Collingwood, Ontario

RIGHT: The steamer *Henry B. Smith* disappeared into oblivion on Lake Superior during the great storm of 1913.

BELOW RIGHT: The steamer *James Carruthers* was was the largest vessel lost in the great storm of 1913.

BOTTOM RIGHT: The steamer *Isaac M. Scott* was lost on Lake Huron during the great storm of 1913. She was found half buried, upside down in the mud in 175 feet of water in 1976.

Wexford

November 9, 1913
Lake Huron

The *Wexford* was one of many "salty" steamers to sail not only the Great Lakes but the oceans of the world; during her 30-year career she had proved her seaworthiness in many a gale. However, on November 9, the ship was headed up Lake Huron when she encountered the height of the great storm. The steamer battled ahead for a short distance, but it was clear that she needed to find shelter. She headed for the safety of Goderich, Ontario, but it was impossible to enter the harbor. The *Wexford*'s master knew the risks involved in entering the narrow passage between breakwaters and most likely thought of the loss of the *Mataafa* (see pages 44–47), when she attempted to enter Duluth at the height of a gale. He decided to turn back into the storm—the result was the same: the *Wexford* foundered that night taking all 17 crewmen with her.

RIGHT: The steel steamer *Wexford* disappeared on Lake Superior during the great storm of 1913.

BELOW RIGHT: The steamer *Argus* was one of seven vessels lost on Lake Huron during the great storm of 1913.

Owner: Western Steamship Company
Builder: William Doxford and Sons Company
Dimensions: 270.0 x 40.0 x 16.6, 2,800 gt.
Built: 1883 at Sunderland, England

Argus

November 9, 1913
Lake Huron

The steel steamer *Argus* passed by Detroit on November 8, 1913, loaded with coal and heading north. A day later she was off Goderich, Ontario, struggling to stay afloat in the storm. The steamer *George C. Crawford* sighted the *Argus* briefly, struggling in the storm, but the *Argus* quickly disappeared under the waves, taking with her all 23 crewmen on board.

Owner: Interlake Steamship Company
Builder: American Shipbuilding Company
Dimensions: 416.0 x 50.0 x 28.0, 7,000 gt.
Built: 1905 at Lorain, Ohio

Northern Queen

November 9, 1913
Lake Huron

The *Northern Queen* left Port Huron on November 9, and after only a few hours sailing was experiencing difficulties. Overpowered, the package steamer headed back to Port Huron, but the extreme weather made the approach to St. Clair River too dangerous for the ship to risk. She was forced to drop anchors, but they failed to hold and she was driven ashore near Kettle Point, Ontario. So close was the stricken ship to land, that witnesses could see the faces of the crew aboard. Later that night, all the crew reached safety and a few days later a salvage crew was able to save the vessel and tow her back to Buffalo, New York, for extensive repairs.

Owner: Northern Steamship Company
Builder: Globe Iron Works Company.
Dimensions: 299.5 x 40.8 x 21.6, 2,476 gt.
Built: 1889 at Cleveland, Ohio

LEFT AND RIGHT: The *Charles S. Price* capsized so quickly that the steward on board was still wearing his apron when he abandoned ship. Some of the bodies from the *Price* were found to be wearing life preservers from the steamer *Regina*.

BELOW LEFT: The steamer *Regina* was another victim of the great storm of 1913 on Lake Huron. Divers discovered the *Regina*'s upside down hull in 1985.

Regina and *Charles S. Price*

November 9, 1913
Lake Huron

By November 13, 1913, when the Great Lakes maritime community was assessing the terrible toll of the storm, the lost souls of two vessels were causing something of a mystery.

On November 9, the steel steamers *Regina* and *Charles S. Price* had been on Lake Huron as the storm struck. It was believed that each had attempted to battle through the heavy seas, but both had been overwhelmed by the storm. However, bodies later began to wash ashore near Sarnia, Ontario, and after they had been identified, it was realized that some of the *Charles S. Price* crewmen were wearing life preservers from the *Regina*. Sailors theorized that the *Price* and *Regina* must have collided and in the confusion some crewmen ended up with lifejackets from the other vessel. However, this theory was dismissed after the *Charles S. Price* was discovered, capsized, on Lake Huron. She was believed to be one of the other many vessels lost at first, but a diver confirmed the steamer's identity and a quick examination revealed that the ship showed no signs of having been involved in a collision. After the wreck of the *Regina* was found in 1985, it was certain that the two vessels had not collided. In what circumstances the ships did meet remains a mystery.

Regina
Owner: Canada Interlake Company
Builder: A. McMillan and Son
Dimensions: 249.7 x 42.6 x 20.5, 1,957 gt.
Built: 1907 at Dumbarton, Scotland

Charles S. Price
Owner: Mahoning Steamship Company
Builder: American Shipbuilding Company
Dimensions: 504.0 x 54.0 x 30.0, 6,322 gt.
Built: 1910 at Lorain, Ohio

William Nottingham

November 10, 1913
Lake Superior

The *William Nottingham*, bound from Port Arthur, Ontario, fully laden with a cargo of Canadian wheat, entered the fray on November 10, 1913. The ship was making for shelter and had nearly made it when she ran aground on a reef near Parisian Island. Having exhausted her coal bunkers the master and crew knew that she would soon lose steam pressure without another fuel source. The resourceful crew found the answer in the holds, using the wheat cargo to keep the boilers going. The *Nottingham* suffered severe damage and the cargo was lost, but the steamer and her crew were rescued.

Owner: United States Transportation Company
Builder: Buffalo Shipbuilding Company
Dimensions: 377.0 x 50.0 x 28.0, 4,234gt.
Built: 1902 at Buffalo, New York

C. F. Curtis, Annie M. Peterson, and Selden E. Marvin

November 18, 1914
Lake Superior

The loss of the steamer *C. F. Curtis* and the schooner-barges *Annie M. Peterson* and *Selden E. Marvin* on November 18, 1914, was a major tragedy for their owner, the Hines Lumber Company. The trio of ships was heading toward the "Soo" on Lake Superior in a strong northwest gale. The *C. F. Curtis* was making no headway and dropped the towlines to the two barges—it is most likely that there was a breakdown in the steamer's machinery. Unable to steer, the *C. F. Curtis* was driven aground on an offshore sandbar near Grand Marais, Michigan, and the waves punished the small wooden steamer until she broke up. The schooner-barge *Annie M. Peterson*, unable to raise any sails, was driven ashore a short distance from *Curtis*. The *Selden E. Marvin* was able to raise some sails for a short period, but also came to grief offshore, some 40 miles east of the *Curtis* and *Peterson*. Several of the crew from these two vessels made it to land. Exhausted and suffering from exposure, all but one collapsed and died on the beach. The desperate survivor traveled some seven miles before death overtook him at the front of the Grand Marais breakwater, where he was later found with his hands stretched out, trying to get over the breakwater.

RIGHT: The wooden steamer *C. F. Curtis* foundered off Grand Marais, Michigan, on Lake Superior in 1914.

BELOW RIGHT: The schooner barge *Selden E. Marvin* shown here with a large deckload. Notice the deckload is higher than the aft deckhouse.

BOTTOM RIGHT: The steel steamer *Choctaw*.

C. F. Curtis
Owner: Hines Lumber Company
Builder: David Lester
Dimensions: 174.0 x 32.4 x 14.0, 532 gt.
Built: 1882 at Marine City, Michigan

Annie M. Peterson
Owner: Hines Lumber Company
Builder: Pete Peterson

Dimensions: 190.5 x 33.0 x 13.0, 631 gt.
Built: 1874 at Fort Howard

Selden E. Marvin
Owner: Hines Lumber Company
Builder: Bailey Bros.
Demensions: 175.0 x 33.0 x 12.0, 618 gt.
Built: 1882 at Toledo, Ohio

Choctaw

July 12, 1915
Lake Huron

A Milwaukee newspaper headlined "Boats Collide and All On Board Lost" after the collision of the steel steamer *Choctaw* with some unknown vessel during the night of July 12, 1915. The report was printed after the steamer *James H. Reed* passed through a field of wreckage on her way to the "Soo" and this information was passed on to the newspapers. Although no bodies were sighted, it was believed that all hands must have drowned, and many families awoke to the news that a father or brother had died in the shipwreck. However, a few days later the steamer *Wacondah* arrived in Port Huron with the entire crew of the *Choctaw* on board. The two ships had collided in heavy fog off Presque Isle, Lake Huron, and the damage to the *Choctaw* was so severe that she sank within five minutes, although all of her crew were able to escape to the *Wacondah*.

Owner: Cleveland Cliffs Iron Company
Builder: Cleveland Shipbuilding Company
Dimensions: 266.9 x 38.1 x 17.9, 1,573 gt.
Built: 1892 at Cleveland, Ohio

Eastland

July 24, 1915
Lake Michigan

On the morning of July 24, 1915, the employees of the Western Electric Company were busily preparing for the annual company picnic. Everyone had dressed in their best clothes and was looking forward to a full day of fun and games. There were plans for races, contests, and a parade, along with a band playing music throughout the festivities. This was to be the grandest celebrations. The whole event was to be held at the largest resort in the Midwest in Michigan City, Indiana.

Weeks earlier, the committee in charge of the gala event had entered into a contract with the Indiana Transportation Company to ferry the expected flocks of people from Chicago over to Michigan City. Five vessels were slated to accommodate the expected number of Western Electric employees. Indiana Transportation Company actually did not own a single vessel, but chartered them when special occasions required it.

The night before the picnic, the committee officials were worried that they did not have enough boats for everyone. The committee's ticket-selling campaign had been so successful that over 7,500 tickets were sold the day before the event—in addition to nearly 9,000 employees attending the picnic. However, the vessels and their sailing times were already announced in the company newspaper. The steamer *Eastland* was the first vessel, scheduled to depart at 7:30 am from the Clark Street Bridge.

Many employees planned to be at the docks by 6:00 am hoping to get to the gala as early as possible; many more still were waiting to board when the *Eastland*'s gangplank was lowered at 6:30 am and boarding began. Passengers rushed aboard, eager to get seats near the railings for a good view of river.

The *Eastland* had recently been licensed to carry up to 2,500 passengers. Only a month before the vessel had been limited to fewer than 2,200 passengers, but the owners persuaded government inspectors to raise the limit up to 2,500. Although each adult who boarded was counted, there were many inconsistencies. Children were not counted and pairs were counted as one adult. The final count of passengers taken aboard the *Eastland* far exceeded the 2,500 allowed.

Just before 7:00 am, there were enough passengers on board the *Eastland* to fill all the seating and views from the railing on the port side of the vessel. This caused the *Eastland* to list to port slightly, a condition which caught the attention of the chief engineer. He immediately opened the seacock on the starboard side to allow more ballast water into the vessel. After a few minutes, the list was corrected and the vessel listed now to starboard. The vessel swung slightly side-to-side, but seemed to straighten out on an even keel.

At 7:15 am, the *Eastland* was making final preparations to depart. The tug *Kenosha* was nearby ready to assist the steamer from the dock, when the *Eastland* lurched sharply to port. Again, the chief engineer had water pumped into the starboard ballast tanks to correct the list. He ordered several men to go on deck to ask the passengers to move over to the starboard side. Very few of them did.

By 7:20 am, the *Eastland*'s second mate was prepared to cast off the stern lines. Just before the captain gave the order to release the lines, the *Eastland* listed further to port. Several crewmen jumped over the railing and onto the dock. Instantly, the captain ordered the doors opened to evacuate the passengers from the *Eastland*, but it was too late. The list kept increasing. Water poured into the open ports, while passengers and furniture alike slid down the slanted deck onto the port side. The *Eastland* finally went over on her side leaving only her white starboard side still above water and only a few hundred people managed to leap onto the exposed side to safety.

Around the *Eastland* were men, women, and children thrashing in the water. Men on the nearby docks threw anything that floated into the water, but it made little difference. Those in the water were frantically trying to stay alive. Some clutched onto others so strongly that some

ABOVE: The passenger steamer *Eastland* shown with passengers along its decks. She was allowed to carry up to 2,500 souls. The *Eastland* was converted to a Naval Reserve training vessel in 1916. Renamed the *Wilmette*, the vessel served through World War II.

pulled from the water had only a shred of clothes left on. Many more pleaded for help, but onlookers could only watch in disbelief. Quickly, the shrieks of those drowning echoed down the river. Vessels rushed to the scene at once. Along with tugs, private yachts, and small launches, one of Chicago's fireboats began to pull survivors out of the water.

Those still trapped in the *Eastland*'s hull suffered a worse fate. Two women were trapped in their stateroom when the vessel overturned. Slowly, the air in the stateroom began to leak out. Water gradually rose higher and higher. They soon gave up hope of being rescued. Not until they heard sledgehammers pounding against the hull, did they realize there was still some hope. Rescuers quickly realized that sledgehammers made little impression on the *Eastland*'s hull and acetylene torches were brought in. Meanwhile, the water had risen nearly up to the necks of the two women. They shrieked and clawed at the hull in vain. As they gasped the last remaining air, the torches cut through the hull. Rescuers pulled them to safety. Both were incoherent, their clothing in shreds and fingernails torn and bleeding.

By midnight, the official death count had reached 810. The Red Cross established a mass morgue at a nearby armory. The morgue stayed open through the night to the public for identification. The newspapers ran an entire page of description of the deceased, but many bodies could not be identified. The Red Cross provided other relief including raising funds for the victims' families. Contributors included the Western Electric Company, the mayor's office, and other citizens of Chicago.

In the wake of the disaster, authorities began investigating the cause for the vessel's sudden capsizing. The *Eastland* was seaworthy with proper equipment in working condition. It had sailed for over 12 years without mishap. Investigators found no fault with the captain and its crew in the handling of the vessel. After all the witnesses testified and experts reviewed the vessel, the investigation revealed no reason why the accident could have happened.

Howver, many sailors stated that the *Eastland* was "crank" when its ballast tanks were empty. This condition refers to instability in a vessel where it would list heavily in turns while the vessel was operating empty. The *Eastland*'s first owners worried enough about this condition to contract out a naval architect to recommend structural changes. After a series of tests, the architect suggested removing the staterooms from the top deck and relocating the engines, but the owners had not acted upon these recommendations.

RIGHT: A view of the capsized *Eastland* at Chicago, Illinois, in 1915. Notice the large numbers of passengers standing on the vessel's side.

LEFT: The barge *Yonkers* was first launched as a wooden package freight steamer in 1879. She was reduced to a barge before being stranded on Lake Erie in 1916.

BELOW LEFT: The wooden steamer *Jay Gould* sank on June 17, 1918, after she sprang a leak while en route to Sandwich, Ontario. Both the *Gould* and her tow barge, *Commodore*, were loaded with coal from Cleveland, Ohio, and were proceeding down Lake Erie when the *Jay Gould*'s hull seams failed, rapidly filling the cargo hold with water, which overwhelmed the bilge pumps. Fortunately, another steamer—the *Midvale*—responded to the *Jay Gould*'s signals for assistance—and the *Jay Gould*'s crew of 22 was able to transfer to the rescuing ship before their own disappeared beneath the waves.

Many offered their opinions as to the cause of the capsizing. John V. Elbert, a crewman, thought the capsizing was the result of the rapid movement of the passengers to the port side. Elbert became the authoritative source for many newspaper reports since he had survived another famous shipwreck, that of the *Titanic*. However, a passenger on board disputed Elbert's hypothesis, stating that everyone was packed aboard too closely to move rapidly from one side of the ship to the other. The passenger also concluded that the reason the vessel overturned was that it was over-capacity. He estimated over 3,500 passengers aboard since every part of the vessel was crowded to standing room only. Investigators dismissed the passenger's claim since the *Eastland* had sailed several years with over 3,300 passengers on board without incident.

The *Eastland* hull was raised and the United States government bought it in 1916. It became a gunboat for use as a Naval Reserve training vessel on the Great Lakes. The vessel was renamed the *Wilmette* and served in the navy without incident. After World War II, the *Wilmette* was decommissioned and sent to the ship breakers in 1948.

The *Eastland* disaster remains as an enigma to this day. The reason the vessel suddenly overturned, killing 835 passengers is still not known.

Owner: St. Joseph and Chicago Steamship Company
Builder: Jenks Shipbuilding Company
Dimension: 265.0 x 38.2 x 19.5, 1,961 gt.
Built: 1903 at Port Huron, Michigan

Yonkers

June 5, 1918
Lake Erie

The barge *Yonkers* was originally launched as the wooden package steamer *Milwaukee* in 1879. After many years in use, the vessel's condition had deteriorated from age, and since reconstruction was economically unfavorable, the steamer was reconstructed into a tow barge in 1911. In 1916, the *Yonkers* was being towed to Ashtabula, Ohio, when she struck an offshore sand bar. Because it was late in the season, salvagers decided to wait until the next year to attempt to free the barge. However, *Yonkers* was left untouched throughout the 1917 season, and started to break apart on the sandbar. Salvors lost interest as many other wrecks were much more profitable than the old wooden barge, and she was left to rot. On June 5, 1918, her fate was finally decided when she caught fire and burned to the waterline. Her remains still sit off Ashtabula on Lake Erie.

Owner: Edward E. Gillen
Builder: Thomas Quayle and Sons
Dimensions: 264.9 x 36.7 x 16.4, 1,770 gt.
Built: 1879 at Cleveland, Ohio

Myron

November 22, 1919
Lake Superior

On November 22, 1919, the wooden steamer *Myron* along with her tow, the schooner barge *Miztec*, were lashed by a northeast gale off Whitefish Point, Lake Superior. Just a few hours earlier, the two vessels had been at Munising, Michigan, loading a cargo of lumber bound for Buffalo, New York. While the vessels were securing the lumber, the *Myron*'s master, Captain Neal, had to make a fateful decision.

LEFT: The twisted remains of the *Chester A. Congdon,* which veered off course and struck Canoe Rocks off Isle Royale, Lake Superior, on November 6, 1918. When the photograph was taken, the stern had already broken off and sunk in deep water.

BELOW LEFT: The steamer *Chester A. Congdon* was originally launched as the *Salt Lake City*—seen here in 1907.

BELOW: Sightseers next to the remains of the wooden steamer *Myron.* This section broke off and floated ashore when the *Myron* sank on Lake Superior in 1919.

Captain Neal had many years of experience on the Great Lakes. He knew that a storm was approaching, but he hoped to reach safety of Whitefish Bay before it caught his vessel, for he knew his aged wooden steamer was in no shape to take the beating of a severe November gale. He considered that the trip to the Whitefish Bay was only 90 miles distant and thought about the valuable cargo and most of all, his crew. But it was close to the end of the shipping season and if the *Myron* delayed departure, she might not be able to reach Buffalo in time. The Great Lakes would soon be choked by ice and a wait of even a day could make the difference between a successful voyage or spending the winter without the usual season bonus.

Captain Neal gave the order to set sail and departed Munising with *Miztec* in tow. Several hours later, the storm struck. Intermittent rain and snow squalls lashed the two vessels and the wind quickly increased up to 30 miles an hour, whipping the waves higher. Both ships were taking equal punishment, but the *Myron* was worse off. Her seams were opening up and the decks were heavily coated in ice. Captain Neal ordered the men to pumps, but they had little effect: water was rising in the *Myron*'s hold and the vessel looked doomed to sink.

Hope for the *Myron* was only a short distance away. The steel steamer *Adriatic* was heading toward Whitefish Bay and caught sight of the *Myron*'s plight. The *Adriatic*'s master, Captain McRae, headed his vessel toward the stricken vessel and pulled close to the *Myron*, staying windward to shield her from the waves. The three vessels proceeded slowly toward Whitefish Bay. But when they were abreast of Vermillion Point, Captain Neal realized that he wouldn't reach safety unless the *Myron* released the towline to the *Miztec*. Neal maneuvered the *Myron* to pull alongside the schooner barge and explained the situation to the barge's captain. They agreed and the *Myron* dropped the towline and the *Miztec* dropped her anchors.

The *Myron* and *Adriatic* continued toward Whitefish Bay with great difficulty. The gale had reached its peak, with winds in excess of 50 miles an hour. Even with the *Adriatic*'s help, the *Myron* was settling lower every minute. When the two vessels were just six miles from safety, the *Myron* suddenly lost power—her boilers had been extinguished by the ingress of water. Captain Neal realized that his vessel was lost and ordered the crew to the lifeboats. He also signaled the *Adriatic* that the vessel was going down. Within a few minutes the *Myron* sank, but the crew had escaped into the lifeboats, albeit without their captain. He was still in the pilothouse when the vessel sank and the pilothouse roof had broken free from the hull. Captain Neal climbed on top of the roof, but it quickly drifted away from the lifeboats.

The plight of the *Myron* had not gone unseen from shore. The Vermillion Coast Guard Station had sighted the distress signals and launched its motor lifeboat. As it approached the point where the *Myron* had gone down, a large field of wreckage blocked the way—the steamer's load of lumber had washed free and now prevented help reaching the survivors.

The *Adriatic* tried to force her way to the boats and got close enough to throw lines, but the survivors could not grasp them. As the lifeboats drifted into shallower water, the *Adriatic* touched bottom. Captain McRae feared losing his vessel and headed back to deeper water.

The *Myron* survivors, numbed by the freezing temperatures, were already suffering from hypothermia and frostbite. Spray from waves froze to their clothes and quickly coated them in ice. Eventually, all the survivors perished before rescuers could reach them. When the Coast Guard recovered the bodies some even had to be chopped free from the ice. All 16 bodies were taken to Sault Ste. Marie where they were thawed at a funeral home. Only the body of Captain Neal was missing.

Miraculously, the captain survived the ordeal. He had spent a full day on top of the pilothouse roof, which acted as a makeshift raft, and had drifted into Whitefish Bay before a steamer spotted him and picked him up. Neal suffered terribly from frostbite; his hands had swelled so large that his rings were no longer visible. But he eventually made a full recovery and sailed again on the Great Lakes. The other survivor was the schooner barge *Miztec.* The vessel rode out the storm at anchor with little damage but the loss of her deck cargo.

Owner: Omer Blodgett
Builder: J. Collister
Dimensions: 186.0 x 33.0 x 14.0, 732 gt.
Built: 1888 at Grand Haven, Michigan

ABOVE: The steamer *Pere Marquette No. 3* shown before she sank. The steamer's hull was crushed by ice on Lake Michigan in 1920. (See page 94)

RIGHT: The crew of the *Pere Marquette No. 3*, who would have to walk across the ice on Lake Michigan to safety.

BELOW RIGHT: The last photograph of the *Pere Marquette No. 3* before she sank. Notice the stern is completely underwater with only the smokestack visible.

ABOVE AND LEFT: The *City of New York*.

Tioga

November 26, 1919
Lake Superior

On July 10, 1890, the package freight steamer *Tioga* was unloading merchandise at her dock on the Chicago River. The crew was busily hauling crates when an explosion erupted from the after hold. One of the crew had been using a lantern there and had ignited gasoline fumes from a nearby motor. The blast completely destroyed the *Tioga*'s after section and left 26 crewmen dead. This was not to be the end of the *Tioga*, however. A few days later, the vessel was towed to Buffalo for repairs, following which she served for another 29 years.

The second tragedy to befall the *Tioga* occurred on November 26, 1919. The steamer became a total loss when she struck a reef off Eagle River, Lake Superior, during a gale, and then slipped off the rocks to be swallowed by the waves.

Owner: Massey Steamship Company
Builder: Union Dry Dock Company
Dimensions: 285.5 x 38.9 x 14.0, 2,085 gt.
Built: 1885 at Buffalo, New York

RIGHT: Shown here is the aftermath of the explosion aboard the steamer *Tioga*. She was repaired and went back into service before being lost on Lake Superior in 1919.

BELOW RIGHT: The steel steamer *Superior City* before she was lost in Whitefish Bay, Lake Superior, in 1920.

Pere Marquette No. 3

March 7, 1920
Lake Michigan

The steam car ferry *Pere Marquette No. 3* was designed for year-round use. The forward part of her bow was reduced, allowing it to run on ice and break it. To strengthen the vessel, a steel arch and heavy steel diagonal strapping were added internally, and the hull was plated up to the main deck. Along with a massive engine, the *Pere Marquette No. 3* seemed staunch enough to withstand winter use. However, on March 7, 1920, the steamer was attempting to enter Ludington, Michigan, when she became stuck solidly in an icefloe. Winds packed the thick ice against the hull and trapped the ferry. The strain of the ice damaged the stern and the *Pere Marquette No. 3* started to take on water, slowly sinking. All on board were rescued and the *Pere Marquette No. 3* would be raised the next summer, but she was never placed back into service.

Owner: Flint and Pere Marquette Railroad
Builder: Detroit Dry Dock Company
Dimension: 190.0 x 32.8 x 12.4, 924 gt.
Built: 1887 at Wyandotte, Michigan

Superior City

August 20, 1920
Lake Superior

For every shipwreck that can be explained, there are many others that have no explanation. On August 20, 1920, the steamer *Superior City* collided with the steamer *Willis L. King* off Whitefish Point, Lake Superior. The two vessels were steaming four miles from each other when each sent a signal. The *Superior City*'s signal was that it would pass on the starboard side of the *Willis L. King*. The *Willis L. King*, however, interpreted the signal that it was to be a pass on the port side. In the confusion, the *Superior City* swung across the *King*, and—

almost farcically—the two ships collided. The collision left the *Superior City* filling with water rapidly, and her crew raced to the stern to launch the lifeboats. However, the icy waters filling the *Superior City* made contact with the hot boilers and a huge explosion resulted. What remained of the *Superior City* went down very quickly. Unfortunately, the explosion occurred right underneath the crewmen launching the lifeboats: 29 perished with only four survivors.

ABOVE: Although a small vessel, the *Lambton* was considered to be a staunch and sturdy craft.

Owner: Pittsburgh Steamship Company
Builder: Cleveland Shipbuilding Company
Dimensions: 429.0 x 50.0 x 24.7, 4,795 gt.
Built: 1898 at Lorain, Ohio

Lambton

April 19, 1922
Lake Superior

The small and durable steamer *Lambton* was launched in 1909 as a lighthouse and buoy tender for the Canadian government and became the vital link for the lighthouses to civilization. Since many of these lights were located in inhospitable areas, the *Lambton* carried the necessary people and supplies to keep these stations in operation. The *Lambton* was always a welcome sight to the lighthouse keepers, except when it brought the lighthouse inspectors and their "white gloves!"

On April 18, 1922, the *Lambton* was completing the loading of supplies at Sault Ste. Marie, Ontario. Onboard were the lighthouse keepers who would be placed on Caribou and Michipicoten Islands. They needed to get their lighthouses in operation since the navigation season had just opened even though Lake Superior was still covered in large ice fields.

Around ten o'clock in the morning, the *Lambton* pulled away from the docks and headed into Whitefish Bay along with two other steamers, *Glenfinnan* and *Glenlivet*. The weather looked more like winter than spring; snow was falling and strong winds gusted across the lake. However, the group of vessels were easily able to traverse the bay into Lake Superior and a few hours later, the *Glenfinnan* and *Glenlivet* headed west, while the *Lambton* turned north toward Caribou and Michipicoten Islands.

The next day Lake Superior was visited by a severe storm with winds of over 60 miles an hour. Snow squalls continued to reduce visibility and Whitefish Bay was choked with pack ice. There was some concern for the small *Lambton*, but she was known to be a rugged little ship, capable of riding out the storm.

Yet on April 20, the steamer *Glenfinnan* reported that the lighthouse on Caribou Island was still not operational. Since the *Lambton* should have delivered the lighthouse keeper several days before, a search for the vessel was initiated and the tug *G. R. Gray* was chartered to conduct it.

As the tug followed along the same course the *Lambton* should have taken, it passed Parisian Island, one of the *Lambton*'s planned ports of call, and noticed its lighthouse was also not in operation. The searchers concluded that heavy ice must have prevented the ship from approaching the island and that the *Lambton* had continued on to the next lighthouse. The tug continued its search for the small steamer, but did not find any trace of wreckage. After five days of searching, the *Lambton* and all onboard were declared lost.

Facts that could explain the loss were eventually forthcoming from the master of the *Glenfinnan*. He reported that the *Lambton* had broken her steering gear and had to rig some lines, but without the proper tackles. He also stated that the *Lambton* had accidentally collided with the *Glenfinnan* when the latter became stuck in an ice field. The *Glenfinnan*'s master was confident that the *Lambton* had taken no damage from the collision, but a thorough inspection could obviously not be conducted while the steamer was fully loaded out on the lake.

It follows then that the *Lambton* encountered a severe storm with a rigged steering and possible damage from an earlier collision. She would have lost control of her steering gear and eventually fallen into the troughs to sink. The steamer also could have been suffereing from a broken a hull plate after the collision with the *Glenfinnan,* and during the storm, water might have poured into her holds until the steamer was waterlogged and sank. All this is, however, conjecture. Since no wreckage was recovered and there were no witnesses, or any conclusive evidence, the loss of the lighthouse tender *Lambton* remains a mystery.

Owner: Ministry of Marine and Fisheries, Canada
Builder: Government Shipyard
Dimensions: 108.0 x 25.1 x 12.7, 323 gt.
Built: 1909 at Sorel, Quebec

Pere Marquette No. 4

May 15, 1923
Lake Michigan

The car ferry *Pere Marquette No. 4* was outbound from Milwaukee, Wisconsin, heading toward Ludington, Michigan on May 15, 1923, in poor conditions with a heavy fog reducing visibility to a few feet. After two hours, the *Pere Marquette No. 4* had traveled some 25 miles into Lake Michigan, but the weather had not improved. Suddenly, another vessel burst out of the fog ahead. The vessel was the *Pere Marquette No. 17*, a sister ship, on the opposite route bound for Milwaukee from Ludington. The two ferries collided head-on with the *No. 4* sustaining most of the damage—a crushed bow and a gaping hole in the hull, fortunately above the waterline. This meant that the *Pere Marquette No. 4* could be

ABOVE: The wooden steamer *Pere Marquette No. 4* shown with a large number of passengers posing for the photograph.

LEFT: The steamer *Pere Marquette No. 4* stuck in winter ice on Lake Michigan. Following her collision with *No. 17* she was converted to a barge. (See page 95)

ABOVE RIGHT: The *Pere Marquette No. 8* shown burning at Marquette, Michigan, in 1927.

RIGHT: The crew of the *Pere Marquette No.4* around 1915. Sitting in front are the first mate, captain, and second mate.

towed to Manistee. While the Pere Marquette Railroad operated a large fleet from a small number of ports, this accident was the only one that saw a collision between two of their vessels.

Owner: Flint and Pere Marquette Railroad
Builder: Detroit Dry Dock Company
Dimensions: 186.6 x 34.5 x 12.4, 941 gt.
Built: 1888 at Wyandotte, Michigan

Orinoco

May 18, 1924
Lake Superior

On May 18, 1924, the wooden steamer *Orinoco* and her tow, the wooden barge *Chieftain*, encountered a strong spring gale. The gale had winds reaching 60 mph along with subfreezing temperatures. In these conditions, the two vessels struggled on Lake Superior to reach shelter of Whitefish Bay. To make matters worse, the *Orinoco* began to leak and take on water. The *Orinoco* battled through the storm, but it was clear the steamer wasn't going to reach safety in time. The master ordered the crew to lifeboats while he and the chief engineer attempted to beach the steamer on nearby Montreal Island. Before *Orinoco* reached shore, she lurched over and sank, taking the master and chief engineer with her. The tug *Gargantua* was in the vicinity and picked up 17 crewmen—tragically, two men died of exposure while in the lifeboats.

Owner: Unavailable
Builder: J. Davidson
Dimensions: 295.0 x 44.0 x 21.0, 2226 gt.
Built: 1898 at West Bay City, Michigan

Clifton

September 21, 1924
Lake Huron

The steamer *Clifton* was launched as a whaleback in 1892 and converted into a self-unloader in 1924. The whaleback design allows water to wash across the deck with the least amount of resistance, but the 1924 conversion gave the *Clifton* a self-unloading boom. This boom acted like a huge barrier and created resistance to wind and waves. While the conversion to self-unloader prolonged the useful life of the *Clifton*—using the self-unloading boom, the *Clifton* could discharge her cargo without the expensive assistance from dockhands—the conversion would also be the cause of her demise. On September 21, 1924, *Clifton* was loaded with stone and despatched from Sturgeon Bay bound for Detroit. She made good progress and reached the straits without any difficulties. However, the weather degraded into a strong southwesterly gale. Wave after wave smashed onto the *Clifton*. Each time a wave rolled onto the deck, it placed more and more stress on the holding lock to the self-unloading boom. Eventually the lock broke free and the boom swung over the side of the *Clifton*. This immediately made the vessel unstable, and she foundered taking all 27 hands down with her.

Owner: Cleveland Cliffs Iron Company
Builder: American Steel Barge Company
Dimensions: 308.0 x 38.0 x 24.0, 1,713 gt.
Built: 1892 at West Superior, Wisconsin

ABOVE: The steamer *Glenlyon* passing through the Soo Locks with its crew relaxing on the stern. Notice the crewman peeking out of an aft porthole.

Glenlyon

October 31, 1924
Lake Superior

The *Glenlyon* left Fort Williams on October 30, 1924, with a cargo of Canadian wheat. It was soon apparent that the conditions were too violent for any vessel, so she headed back into Thunder Bay, Lake Superior, to wait for better weather. By late October 31, the gale seemed to have let up, and the *Glenlyon* continued on her way. However, the gale renewed in ferocity and struck the steamer off Isle Royale. Beset by winds and waves, the *Glenlyon* headed for shelter, but struck an unknown shoal off Menagerie Island. The impact tore open the steamer's hull, and soon she was completely flooded. The crew sent out a distress message by radio, and two of her sister ships responded. Soon, the *Glenlyon*'s crewmen were rescued. Over the next month, salvagers attempted to free the *Glenlyon*, but the steamer was too badly damaged and any work would have to wait till spring. When they arrived after winter, storms had forced the *Glenlyon* off the shoal where she sank.

Owner: Great Lakes Transportation Company
Builder: F. W. Wheeler and Company
Dimensions: 328.0 x 42.5 x 20.5, 2,759 gt.
Built: 1893 at West Bay City, Michigan

Turret Crown

November 2, 1924
Lake Huron

As with so many vessels that plied the Great Lakes, the Turret Crown was no stranger to mishaps. Her first was on November 27, 1906, when she ran aground off Grand Marais, Michigan, when her intoxicated master lost his bearings and drove the vessel ashore. Eighteen years later, *Turret Crown* was caught in a storm and the master attempted to reach safety behind Manitoulin Island. The vessel ran hard aground on the north side of the island while still exposed to the storm. Waves punished the *Turret Crown* breaking it in two. A total loss, the remains were later cut for scrap.

Owner: Coastwise Steamship and Barge Company
Builder: William Doxford and Sons
Dimensions: 253.0 x 44.0 x 19.4, 1,851 gt.
Built: 1895 at Sunderland, England

RIGHT: The steamer *Turret Crown* went aground on Manitoulin Island, Lake Huron in 1924.

BELOW AND BOTTOM RIGHT: The steamer *Lakeland* begins to settle lower as water fills the stern and finally sinks beneath the waves. In 1979 an automobile was salvaged from her holds.

Lakeland

December 2, 1924
Lake Michigan

The *Lakeland* was deemed the fastest package freighter on the Great Lakes soon after she was fitted out in 1887, surpassing the freighter, *Tioga*. Originally launched as the *Cambria*, in 1901 she was sold to the Port Huron and Duluth Steamship Company, where she was converted to include passenger service by the addition of a single deck of staterooms, cabins, and a dining saloon above the main deck. During the summer season, the renamed *Lakeland* made regular trips from Port Huron to Duluth with its complement of passengers. After the passenger season closed, she also made special trips carrying automobiles. On Tuesday, December 2, 1924, the *Lakeland* had just finished delivering a cargo of automobiles to Chicago, and was heading back towards Detroit. That night, the winds picked up from the northwest, forcing the *Lakeland* to seek shelter of Sturgeon Bay, Wisconsin.

On December 3, the winds moderated and the *Lakeland* continued on her way. Only a few miles offshore, however, the officers were alerted that the ship was leaking badly. Although they quickly ordered the pumps started and headed back to Sturgeon Bay, it soon became clear that the *Lakeland* would not make it back to shore before she foundered. Her master ordered an SOS to be sent out. A car ferry, *Ann Arbor No. 6*, responded immediately and all 26 crewmen were rescued.

Owner: W. A. Hawgood
Builder: Globe Iron Works, Company
Dimensions: 280.0 x 40.0 x 20.0, 2,425 gt.
Built: 1887 at Cleveland, Ohio

City of Bangor

November 30, 1926
Lake Superior

Lake Superior's coastline is notorious for its isolation. A small number of hamlets dot the southern shore; even fewer can be found on the northern. One of the most isolated areas lies

ABOVE: A view of the stern of the *City of Bangor*. The steamer could not be pulled free and was abandoned by her owners.

LEFT: The cargo of Chrysler automobiles being unloaded from the stranded *City of Bangor*. The cars were driven over the ice to shore.

around the Keweenaw Point. Surrounded by the lake on three sides, its rugged, rocky shore is a formidable place to be stranded, especially in the winter months. The steel steamer *City of Bangor* encountered this shore on November 30, 1926. She was headed for Duluth with 248 new Chrysler automobiles on board. Although there was no room left to put another automobile on deck or below in the hold, the *Bangor* was drawing less than usual. Most steamers prefer to have a lower profile in the water, to allow the screw to have more "bite," and also to present a smaller area against the waves and wind. The *Bangor* struggled to find shelter when the storm overtook the vessel on November 30. With her high profile, the wind and waves pounded her sides till she ran ashore off Keweenaw Point. The *Bangor*'s crew was rescued shortly after, but her cargo of automobiles was another problem. Since there were no roads and snowdrifts could easily exceed ten feet in height, it would take several weeks and hard effort to salvage the automobiles from Keweenaw Point. However, the winter weather came to the rescue, and with the aid of a snowplow, and taking advantage of the annual lake freeze, 230 automobiles were recovered by creating a roadway over the iced-up lake.

Owner: Nicholson Transit Company
Builder: F. W. Wheeler
Dimensions: 444.5 x 44.8 x 23.5, 4,202 gt.
Built: 1896 at West Bay City, Michigan

RIGHT: The small passenger and freight steamer *America* stranded off Isle Royale, Lake Superior in 1928.

BELOW RIGHT: A view of the *America* partially sunk off Isle Royale. Salvage attempts in 1966 failed when someone dynamited the wreck.

America

June 7, 1928
Lake Superior

The small excursion steamer *America* was lost during the early hours of June 7, 1928, on her regular run along Isle Royale. The vessel was traveling out of Washington Harbor when a large thud shuddered her hull. The *America* had struck a reef and began to fill with water. One of the many passengers onboard was Lyman Clay. He and his family were traveling from their summer cabin to Grand Portage, Minnesota. When Clay and other passengers emerged from their cabins, the crew told them that they would have to get into the lifeboats. However, he did not think there was anything seriously wrong until he reached the main deck, where he was surrounded by the rest of the crew and passengers. At this point the *America* lurched to one side.

Before Clay reached the safety of the lifeboats, he realized that the family dog was still tied to the stern post behind the dining room. He asked a crewman if he could go back and retrieve the dog and the crewman ventured down the passageway a short distance. But the ship was listing further and the crewman was forced back as a wall of water rushed out of the passageway—by the time he reached Clay, it had risen to their waists. The latter then heard someone calling for everyone to go up to the lifeboats on the hurricane deck.

The first two lifeboats were lowered from the davits, but were crushed as the vessel lurched again to the other side. Clay along with the other passengers now had to go down below again to reach the opposite side and the other lifeboats. Once this was achieved, crew and passengers quickly jumped into the boats that had already been lowered, only to find that the plugs were still pulled out, causing more consternation while they were found and replaced. Not until the lifeboats had pulled away from the *America* did Clay and the rest of the passengers realize how far the vessel had already sunk. Nearly two-thirds of the stern was underwater. It had only been half an hour from that first thud. The lifeboats rowed across the bay to a fisherman's dock where they landed safely.

In 1965, a Duluth salvage team planned an attempt to raise the steamer using compressed air containers. But shortly before work commenced, someone dynamited the wreck, preventing any further attempts to salvage the *America*.

Owner: Booth Fisheries
Builder: Detroit Dry Dock Company
Dimensions: 164.6 x 31.0 x 11.0, 486 gt.
Built: 1898 at Wyandotte, Michigan

RIGHT: The schooner *Our Son* sailing without cargo. Note the deterioration of the hull.

Yorkton

July 11, 1930
Lake Superior

The canal steamer *Yorkton* collided with steamer *Mantadoc* one mile off Whitefish Point. While the *Mantadoc* received minor damage, the *Yorkton* hull was punctured. Water rushed into the *Yorkton*'s holds, but the steamer was able to reach shallow waters before she sank. The *Yorkton* was raised later, but would be wrecked again on June 20, 1936 when she went ashore near Gargantua Harbor, Ontario, on Lake Superior. She was later released by the tug *Favorite*, repaired, and then sold for off-lake use.

Owner: Mathews Steamship Company
Builder: Sunderland Shipbuilding Company
Dimensions: 250.0 x 42.7 x 16.4, 1,772 gt.
Built: 1911 at Sunderland

Our Son

September 25, 1930
Lake Michigan

One of the last two schooners still in use on the Great Lakes, on September 25, 1930, the *Our Son* was headed to Muskegon, Michigan with a cargo of pulpwood. The weather was fair, and with the fresh breeze the schooner could have reached port by the next day. That night the winds increased in force, whipping the waves into a frenzy. The wind ripped the sails away leaving only bare masts. Without any headway, *Our Son* fell into the trough of the heavy seas. The schooner's aged hull began to show stress, and water leaked into the cargo hold. Her master was realistic about the situation. He knew that the vessel was doomed, but he knew all aboard would be lost if they abandoned ship into the small yawl. Without radio or wireless, the schooner was isolated and in near-sinking condition. All on board could only pray for rescue. Their prayers were answered the following day, when the steamer *William Nelson* appeared in the distance. The *Nelson* steamed for the schooner, and with some daring maneuvering, pulled alongside *Our Son* allowing the schooner's crew to jump over to the deck of the *Nelson* to safety. Shortly afterward, the waterlogged *Our Son* took its final plunge to the bottom.

Owner: W. Schlosser
Builder: Henry Kelley
Dimensions: 182.0 x 35.0 x 14.0, 720 gt.
Built: 1875 at Lorain, Ohio

George M. Cox

May 23, 1933
Lake Superior

On May 23, 1933, the passenger steamer *George M. Cox* left on her inaugural voyage under the Isle Royale Transportation Company. The vessel had been purchased by George M. Cox who planned to operate two vessels between Chicago, Illinois, and Fort William, Ontario. Mr. Cox and 18 close friends, were the only passengers onboard.

The *Cox* made good progress and reached Houghton, Michigan, on the afternoon of May 28. After passage through the Keweenaw waterway, she set course for Rock of Ages Light. There she made a final course adjustment towards Fort William and the captain ordered the engines at full speed, pushing the ship's speed to nearly 17 knots. Although Lake Superior was calm, visibility was reduced due to increasing fog. Nevertheless, in the afternoon, the *Cox*'s master handed the watch over to the first mate.

ABOVE, LEFT, AND ABOVE RIGHT: The passenger steamer *George M. Cox* impaled herself on rocks off Isle Royale, Lake Superior in 1933 during its first cruise for its new owners. These views show the stricken vessel nearly awash.

Around 6:30 p.m., while some of the passengers were sitting down for the evening meal, a large thud rang through the vessel. Tables and chairs slid across the floor crashing into bulkheads and the ship's nurse was thrown against a door and stunned. The stewardess helped her to her feet only to be knocked down herself with a second thud. The steamer lurched and began to list heavily to port. She had run aground on Rock of Ages reef. The force of the impact was so severe that the *Cox*'s bow was lifted completely out of the water into the air. The master ordered the wireless to send out an SOS.

There was little panic among the crew and passengers while the lifeboats were being lowered and, after a few hours, all were safely landed to the nearby Rock of Ages Lighthouse. However, the lighthouse could not hold all 120 of them, so many had to take turns waiting outside. It wasn't until 4 a.m. that the steamer Morris Tremaine arrived to pick up the survivors.

The official report stated that the loss of the *George M. Cox* was due to an error while changing course. It was alleged that the first mate had become disorientated in the fog and turned the vessel towards the reef. During the investigation, he was also accused of leaving his post and, while abandoning ship, of leaving the vessel with only one passenger in his lifeboat. When the mate was questioned about his actions he became so irate that he slammed his fists onto a table, shouting that he was being framed. He was so enraged that he started a fight with the marine superintendent of the line when they met in a hotel lobby afterward.

During a following fall gale, the steamer *George M. Cox* broke in two and slipped off the reef.

Owner: Isle Royale Transportation Company
Builder: Craig Shipbuilding Company
Dimensions: 259.0 x 40.5 x 26.6, 1,762 gt.
Built: 1901 at Toledo, Ohio

Henry Cort

November 30, 1934
Lake Michigan

The steamer *Midvale* rammed the whaleback steamer *Henry Cort* near the entrance of the Detroit River on April 24, 1918. The *Henry Cort* suffered severe damage and sank in 30 feet of water. Salvagers went to work to raise the vessel, and by October 17, the *Cort* had been raised and was towed to Conneaut, where she was repaired. The *Cort* sailed for a few more years before she had another accident, striking the breakwater at Muskegon harbor in Lake Michigan.

On November 30, 1934, the *Henry Cort* was traveling light on Lake Michigan in a heavy fall gale. The *Cort*'s master sought shelter at Muskegon, but the whaleback was driven into the breakwater before she could enter the harbor. Lifesavers responded and rescued all aboard, although one lifesaver was killed when he slipped off the breakwater and drowned. Over the winter, storms continued to pound the *Henry Cort*. Eventually, she broke in two and sank.

Owner: Pittsburg Steamship Company
Builder: American Steel Barge Company
Dimensions: 320.0 x 42.0 x 25.0, 2,234 gt.
Built: 1892 at Superior, Wisconsin

ABOVE: *Henry Cort* suffered two shipwrecks in its life, sinking first in 1917 and then again in 1934. Here the steamer is seen in 1917 off Par Point. She would be raised the next year.

ABOVE RIGHT: The 1934 accident—here, the crew of the *Henry Cort* are being rescued. Notice the man crossing over the lake in a breeches buoy.

RIGHT: The remains of the whaleback *Henry Cort* off the breakwater at Muskegon, Michigan, on Lake Michigan in 1934.

ABOVE: The passenger steamer *Tashmoo* seen on the bottom at the docks at Amherstburg, Ontario. The steamer was raised and sold for scrap.

LEFT: The *Lyman Davis*.

Aycliffe Hall

June 11, 1936
Lake Erie

On June 11, 1936, the steel steamer *Aycliffe Hall* collided with the steamer *Edward J. Berwind*. The two vessels were west of Long Point on Lake Erie in heavy fog when the *Berwind* cut deep into the *Aycliffe Hall*'s hull. The *Aycliffe Hall* began to fill rapidly with water and sank minutes later. Luckily, no lives were lost.

Owner: Hall Corporation of Canada
Builder: Smiths Dock Company
Dimensions: 253.0 x 44.1 x 18.5, 1,900 gt.
Built: 1928 at South Bank on Tees, England

Tashmoo

June 18, 1936
Detroit River

Advertised as a refreshing trip, full of time to daydream, the excursion steamer *Tashmoo* ferried passengers along the Detroit and St. Clair River. On June 18, 1936, the *Tashmoo* was traveling down the Detroit River with 1,400 passengers on board when it struck a rock obstruction. Going at full speed, the *Tashmoo*'s hull had ripped open leaving a large hole. The sinking *vessel* headed instantly for shore and was near the Ontario shoreline when she sank in shallow water. All 1,400 passengers and crew were safely taken off the steamer. The damage to the *Tashmoo* was so severe that the steamer was sold for scrap.

Owner: White Star Line
Builder: Detroit Dry Dock
Dimensions: 302.9 x 37.6 x 13.6, 1,344 gt.
Built: 1900 at Wyandotte, Michigan

Neebing

September 24, 1937
Lake Superior

On September 24, 1937, the veteran steamer *Neebing* was towing her usual burden, a gravel barge, through the Nipigon Straits along the northern shore of Lake Superior. Although the seas were rough, the two vessels were in no difficulties when, without warning, the steamer's boilers burst. The resulting explosion instantly sank the *Neebing*, taking five crewmen with her. Another nine crewmen barely escaped with their lives, being rescued by the gravel barge or swimming ashore.

Owner: Sin-Mac Line
Builder: Craig
Dimensions: 193.0 x 40.0 x 15.0, 908 gt.
Built: 1892 at Toledo, Ohio

Islet Prince

July 17, 1938
Lake Huron

On July 17, 1938, the small wooden steamer *Islet Prince* left the docks at Chantry Island preparing to make the short crossing on Lake Huron to Southampton, Ontario. Only a short distance from the docks, the *Islet Prince* ran aground. To free herself, the steamer needed to use all the power its engine could muster. Before enough steam pressure had built up, a fire erupted out of the engine room and engulfed the steamer's upper works. Quickly, the *Islet Prince* was ablaze and it burned to its waterline. No lives were lost, but the steamer was completely destroyed.

Owner: John Tackaberry
Builder: Henry B. Burger
Dimensions: 105.0 x 24.5 x 8.0, 245 gt.
Built: 1902 at Manitowoc, Wisconsin

City of Port Huron

April 8, 1939
Lake Huron

LEFT: The small passenger ferry *City Of Port Huron* sank at her dock in 1939. Taken in 1938, this is one of the last photos of the ferry in operation.

Today they are part of global transportation routes, but in the nineteenth century the Great Lakes were just a major obstacle. There were no bridges, only small ferries. The ferries served as local commuter routes carrying passengers across the many rivers and bays separating nearby towns. The ferry *City of Port Huron* was built for this purpose. In 1891, the ferry operated between Duluth, Minnesota, and Superior, Wisconsin. When the railroad linked the two towns, the ferry was sold and placed into use in other small ports. In 1925, she was sold again to ferry passengers between Port Huron and Sarnia, Ontario. Until 1938, when the new Blue Waters Bridge was erected, the ferry shuttled passengers across the St. Clair River. Finally, on April 8, 1939, the *City of Port Huron* sank at her dock, ending the era of the small ferries.

Owner: Port Huron and Sarnia Ferry Company
Builder: Cleveland Dry Dock Company
Dimensions: 98.0 x 29.9 x 10.0, 183 gt.
Built: 1890 at Cleveland, Ohio

Arlington

May 1, 1940
Lake Superior

BELOW: The steamer *Arlington* foundered on Lake Superior during a violent gale in 1940. She is shown as the *Glencadam* before being renamed in 1939.

The steel steamer *Arlington* foundered in a heavy gale near Superior Shoal on Lake Superior on May 1, 1940. The *Arlington* had loaded a cargo of wheat from Fort William, Ontario, bound for Owen Sound. The steamer headed out toward the middle of Lake Superior instead of the lee of the north shore. The storm was too much for her and she began to sink. All the

crew except the master abandoned to the lifeboats. The steamer *Collingwood* soon rescued them, but the master followed the old tradition of refusing to give up his sinking ship and went down with the vessel.

Owner: Burke Towing and Salvage Company
Builder: Detroit Shipbuilding Company
Dimensions: 244.0 x 43.0 x 18.2, 1,870 gt.
Built: 1913 at Wyandotte, Michigan

Anna C. Minch

November 11, 1940
Lake Michigan

On November 11, 1940, the steamer *Anna C. Minch* was proceeding down Lake Michigan as a severe storm swept over the lake. Wind gusts exceeded 70 mph with waves topping 35 feet. The *Minch* struggled to stay afloat in these conditions, and when she reached Ludington, Michigan, the strain of the storm proved too much for the vessel. In the storm's fury, the steamer developed a large crack which expanded across its hull. Suddenly, the *Minch* broke in two, the bow section quickly drifting away and sanking. The stern stayed afloat for a little longer, drifting a bit further before it also sank. All 24 crewmen perished.

Owner: Kinsman Transit Company
Builder: American Shipbuilding Company
Dimensions: 380.0 x 50.0 x 28.0, 4,285 gt.
Built: 1903 at Cleveland, Ohio

BELOW: The steamer *Anna C. Minch* sank off Pentwater, Michigan, during the same storm that the steamer *William B. Davock* was lost.

RIGHT: On November 11, 1940, the steamer *William B. Davock* foundered in the same storm as that which sank the *Anna C. Minch*. The *Davock* was nearly four hours ahead of the *Minch*, sailing down Lake Michigan when it disappeared. The steamer did not carry a wireless so no distress signal was sent. All 32 crewmen perished, and so one can but guess at the conditions aboard before the vessel foundered. Mountainous waves would have crashed over the deck until, eventually, one or more hatch covers gave way under the strain allowing water to flood into the holds. Slowly, the *Davock* would have lost buoyancy and plunged beneath the waves.

Novadoc

November 11, 1940
Lake Michigan

On November 11, 1940, the steamer *Novadoc* left Chicago with a cargo of powdered coke bound for Fort William, Ontario. The weather was unusually clear and calm as she headed north along Lake Michigan and Captain Steip set course along the Michigan shoreline. This was the shorter route up Lake Michigan, but offered little protection from the weather.

Before the *Novadoc* left Chicago, weather reports predicted a severe storm approaching the Great Lakes. Two weather systems had collided forming a cyclone of immense strength. Captain Steip like many sailors took the weather reports with a grain of salt. Some captains preferred to use their own best judgment on approaching weather.

But by late afternoon, when the *Novadoc* was off Muskegon, Michigan, she was struck by severe winds and rain. Captain Steip had gambled on the weather and lost.

The winds howled against the *Novadoc* while rain and hail blinded Captain Steip's view of the Michigan shoreline. He knew that his vessel was in a precarious situation since she was only a few hundred yards offshore. While other vessels were able to steer into the storm, the *Novadoc* was unable to make the turn into the wind. Captain Steip attempted several times to make the turn, but each time the *Novadoc* failed to respond.

By dusk, the storm had increased in strength. Winds reached gusts over 60 miles an hour while the temperature dropped nearly 40 degrees. Along the shoreline, roofs were ripped off buildings, trees uprooted, and communications were utterly wrecked. In these conditions, the *Novadoc* was slowly being driven closer to shore. Captain Steip knew his vessel would run aground and alerted the crew to prepare them for the worst.

Before midnight, the *Novadoc* finally struck an offshore sandbar and ran aground. The waves crashed over the vessel's decks making any hope of reaching land impossible. The captain knew that the only way his crew was to survive would be if help arrived from shore and he launched several flares during the night, but the weather prevented them being seen.

Unknown to Captain Steip, however, his vessel had been spotted by the Little Sable Point lighthouse keeper. The keeper attempted to signal the *Novadoc* with a lamp, but it was too weak to be seen through the storm. The keeper then rushed to the Ludington Coast Guard Station to notify them a steamer had stranded offshore.

The next morning was a little better than the night before. The storm had not diminished. On the *Novadoc*, Captain Steip along with the crew tried to spot any sign of rescuers, but their attention soon shifted to the vessel itself. The strain from the storm had caused the hull to sag and soon after it broke and the steamer lost power and heating. Two panicked crewmen attempted to abandon to the lifeboats. They crossed over the open deck, but were washed overboard by an enormous wave. Captain Steip and his crew were now without heat or food.

Another day passed, and the crew of the *Novadoc* waited for rescue. When the vessel first wrecked, the crew worried that she would break apart before they could be rescued, but now they were more concerned that they would freeze to death in the numbing cold. The crew had spent nearly 36 hours without heat or food within sight of shore and they had little time left unless rescuers arrived quickly.

Captain Steip was shocked when he caught sight of a small fish tug steaming toward the *Novadoc*. Help was at hand at last. The fish tug *Three Brothers* had ventured into the storm under the command of Captain Cross who had decided that the rescue should not be delayed any further. Cross headed his vessel out to the stricken *Novadoc* and was able to save the remaining 17 crewmen.

While Captain Cross and the crew of the *Three Brothers* were later cited for their bravery, the Coast Guard received accusations of failing to perform its basic function. Feelings ran high between the station's personnel and the local fishermen and rumors spread that the Coast Guard had diverted its attentions to another stranded vessel that was in no danger, but vital to the local economy. Captain Steip and the crew of the *Novadoc* were outspoken in their thanks to the fishermen who rescued them.

Owner: Paterson Steamship Line
Builder: Swan, Hunter & Wigham
Dimensions: 235.0 x 43.0 x 20.0, 1934 gt.
Built: 1928 at Newcastle, England

Admiral and *Cleveco*

December 2, 1942
Lake Erie

Weather on Lake Erie can be disastrous for unwary vessels. The shape and depth of Lake Erie can whip up large waves even in a small storm. On December 2, 1942, two vessels encountered such waves. The tug *Admiral* and the barge *Cleveco* left Toledo bound for Cleveland with 800,000 gallons of oil on board the *Cleveco*. At first, the two vessels made good progress through the snow squalls. However, at 4:00 am the *Admiral* suddenly foundered without any warning. There was no distress signal, flares, or a plea for help over the radio. The *Cleveco* was not even aware the *Admiral* had foundered until the crew realized the towline was pointed straight down into Lake Erie. Alarmed at the situation, the *Cleveco* radioed for assistance. The Coast Guard sent out several motor lifeboats, which searched, along with several tugs, for the *Cleveco*. But before the rescue vessels could reach her, she too would founder taking all hands aboard.

Admiral
Owner: Cleveland Tankers
Builder: Manitowoc Shipbuilding Company
Dimensions: 93.3 x 22.1 x 11.7, 130 gt.
Built: 1922 at Manitowoc, Wisconsin

Cleveco
Owner: Cleveland Tankers
Builder: American Shipbuilding Company
Dimensions: 250.0 x 43.0 x 26.0, 2,441 gt.
Built: 1913 at Lorain, Ohio

RIGHT: The tanker barge *Cleveco* was lost off Cleveland, Ohio, on Lake Erie during a severe storm. The barge was last sighted by the Coast Guard before it disappeared from sight taking all 18 crew with her.

BELOW RIGHT: The tug *Admiral* was reconditioned a few months before it suddenly sank on Lake Erie in 1942.

BOTTOM RIGHT: The remains of the *Hamonic* being towed to the ship breakers for scrap. Many steamship enthusiasts consider the passenger steamer to be one of the finest looking ever to sail the Great Lakes. However, she met disaster the night of July 17, 1945. The *Hamonic* was docked at a warehouse a few miles above Sarnia, Ontario, waiting to load cargo. In the early morning, dockhands began their work, loading merchandise and freight. They used a gas engine to run a conveyor, but when it was started, flames shot out of the motor. Soon the dock was ablaze and the conflagration soon got out of control. Quickly, the flames leaped across to the decks of the *Hamonic* and ignited the *Hamonic*'s wooden works. Although the smoke and flames engulfed the *Hamonic*, cool heads prevailed on board. Of the 230 passengers and crew, incredibly not a single life was lost.

Emperor

June 4, 1947
Lake Superior

On the night of June 4, 1947, the steel steamer *Emperor* finished loading over 10,000 tons of iron ore from the docks at Port Arthur, Ontario, with the first mate, James Morrey, supervising the loading until the last ton dropped from the chutes into the holds. By the time all the cargo hatches had been secured and the *Emperor* pulled away from the docks, it was nearly 11 pm, giving Morrey only one hour of rest before starting his watch.

Around midnight, Morrey relieved Captain Walkinshaw, and as the captain left the wheel-house the first mate set a course around Isle Royale. However, he was so exhausted from his other responsibilities that he steered the *Emperor* off course. Morrey had made a sighting from the wrong lighthouse, putting the ship on a direct course for Canoe Rocks off Isle Royale. However, he was completely unaware of his mistake and soon fell asleep in a chair in the wheelhouse. Meanwhile, the *Emperor* continued toward danger.

It was after 4 am when the vessel crashed to a halt. Crewmen hastily rushed up on deck and a SOS was sent out as the *Emperor* sank. The crew managed to launch two lifeboats just as the ship made a final lurch. One had its plug pop out, leaving its ten occupants in knee-deep water, but the other lifeboat was even less lucky, being pulled under by the suction as the *Emperor* slipped underwater. When it surfaced, four men were able to hang onto its over-turned hull. Several other men were able to swim over to nearby rocks, but 12 did not survive, including Captain Walkinshaw and First Mate Morrey.

The *Emperor*'s distress signal was received by the Coast Guard, which dispatched the cutter *Kimball* to search for survivors. The *Kimball* arrived an hour later and proceeded to rescue 14 men from the lifeboats along with seven men perched on the rocks.

Owner: Canada Steamship Lines
Builder: Collingwood Shipbuilding Company
Dimensions: 525.0 x 56.0 x 31.0, 7,031 gt.
Built: 1911 at Collingwood, Ontario

Noronic

September 15, 1949
Lake Ontario

On September 15, 1949, the passenger steamer *Noronic* started on a special fall cruise to Toronto, Ontario. After picking up passengers in Detroit and Cleveland, the *Noronic* sailed down Lake Erie and through the Welland Canal into Lake Ontario, stopping at Toronto overnight. Many passengers disembarked to go sightseeing or shopping. Some crew left the vessel as well, leaving a small number to serve the passenger needs. By midnight, most of the passengers were asleep in their cabin. However, an hour later, an alarm sounded. A passenger discovered smoke coming out of a locked linen closet. When it was opened, the interior was found to be ablaze, and the crewmen aboard were unable to stop the fire. Soon the vessel was an inferno. The crew helped frantic passengers escape the flames, but 116 lives were lost. The remains of the *Noronic* were pulled from the dock and sold for scrap.

Owner: Northern Navigation Company
Builder: Western Dry Dock and Shipbuilding Company
Dimensions: 362.0 x 52.0 x 24.8, 6,905 gt.
Built: 1913 at Port Arthur, Ontario

Sachem

December 18, 1950
Lake Erie

LEFT: The steamer *Noronic* was one of the largest passenger steamers to operate on the Great Lakes. She caught fire at Toronto, Ontario, in 1949. (See page 123)

BELOW LEFT: The steamer *Henry Steinbrenner* was considered a total loss when it sank after a collision in 1909. In fact she would later be raised and continued for many years until she was lost in a storm on Lake Superior in 1953.

BOTTOM LEFT: The steel steamer *Scotiadoc* was originally launched as the *Martin Mullen* in 1904. The *Scotiadoc* ended its career in a collision in 1953.

The small tug *Sachem* was designed to perform tough work towing barges and dredges across Lake Erie. On December 18, 1950, the tug headed out from Buffalo to the nearby port of Dunkirk. There she was to pick up the scow *Ohio* and tow it to Detroit. However, the *Sachem* never reached Dunkirk or any other port. Several searches by Coast Guard cutters *Tupelo* and *Acacia* found no trace of the tug and its 12-man crew. A week later, wreckage from the *Sachem* was spotted off Silver Creek, New York. There the submerged tug was discovered. Divers were sent down to investigate, but came back with more questions than answers. There were no bodies found on the wreck or any evidence of damage. Also, all the life preservers had been removed from the storage locker, but the emergency alarm switch was not turned on. Investigators concluded that the *Sachem* was suddenly swamped and foundered by a large wave, but admitted that this was only a theory. Only the 12 men who perished aboard her knew the exact cause to the sinking of the *Sachem*.

Owner: Dunbar and Sullivan
Builder: Benjamin T. Cowles
Dimensions: 71.1 x 20.1 x 10.5, 100 gt.
Built: 1907 at Buffalo, New York

Henry Steinbrenner

May 11, 1953
Lake Superior

The early morning of May 10, 1953, the steel steamer *Henry Steinbrenner* pulled away from the iron ore docks at Superior, Wisconsin. Forecasts predicted a few thunderstorms and increasing winds up to 35 mph. The *Steinbrenner* headed down Lake Superior, but the weather was far from what had been forecasted. By May 11, a full raging gale crashed over the *Steinbrenner* with waves 20 to 30 feet high. The steamer's hatch covers began to fail one by one, allowing the heavy seas to pour into the holds. Although the bilge pumps were started, they were unable to stop the holds from flooding further. An SOS was sent out and the order given to abandon ship. The steamer *Joseph H. Thompson* rescued five crewmen on a liferaft and the steamer *D. M. Clemson* rescued another seven crewmen in a lifeboat. However, 17 crewmen perished when the *Steinbrenner* foundered off Isle Royale. Investigators believed that failure of the hand-tightened hatch covers were the direct cause for the steamer's demise.

Owner: Kinsman Transit Company
Builder: Jenks Ship Building
Dimensions: 427.0 x 50.0 x 28.0, 4345 gt.
Built: 1901 at Port Huron, Michigan

Scotiadoc

June 20, 1953
Lake Superior

The Canadian steamer *Scotiadoc* pulled out of Port Arthur, Ontario, with 234,000 bushels of wheat. She traveled a few miles into Thunder Bay when the steamer *Burlington* struck her amidships. Severely damaged, the *Scotiadoc*'s crew scrambled on deck and quickly launched the lifeboats. In the haste to abandon ship, a lifeboat capsized and one crewman drowned; the other 29 crewmen were picked up by the *Burlington*.

Owner: Paterson Steamship Lines
Builder: American Shipbuilding Company
Dimensions: 416.0 x 50.0 x 28.0, 4,635 gt.
Built: 1904 at Cleveland, Ohio

RIGHT: A view of the stern of the steamer *Carl D. Bradley*. The *Bradley* was the flagship of the Bradley Transportation Line Fleet.

Carl D. Bradley

November 17, 1958
Lake Michigan

The last trip of the season is always welcomed by sailors, as it was by those aboard the *Carl D. Bradley*. They wanted to see the year behind them and were looking forward to spending the winter layover with their families and friends. The *Carl D. Bradley* had completed 45 trips during the 1958 navigation season and had only one trip in November left to complete.

The *Carl D. Bradley* was launched in 1927 at Lorain, Ohio. Her hull was made up of steel plates riveted together. At 640 feet in length, the *Bradley* was the longest vessel in service on the Great Lakes at that time. In 1929, she passed another milestone by carrying the largest single cargo up to that time—18,114 tons of limestone from Calcite, Michigan, to Gary, Indiana. If the same cargo had been carried overland, it would have required over 300 railcars.

The *Bradley* left Rogers City, Michigan, with a cargo of limestone bound for Buffington, Indiana. On board her master, Captain Roland Bryan, headed his vessel around the Straits of Mackinac into Lake Huron. Captain Bryan had been in command of the *Bradley* since 1954 and had served aboard other vessels in the company fleet. He was a veteran of many years having first gone to sea at age fourteen. He knew his vessel and what he could expect from it. In letters to friends, Captain Bryan stated his concern for the condition of the *Bradley*. Two weeks before, she had struck bottom at Cedarville, Michigan, rupturing a hull plate. Several bulkheads were rusty and ballast tanks were constantly leaking, requiring pumps to be in operation at all times. However, the vessel had been deemed seaworthy, and was still young enough to have a major refit—a new cargo hold—planned for the winter lay up.

The *Bradley* reached Buffington and her cargo of limestone was quickly discharged. At 6:30 pm on November 17, 1958, she headed back empty up Lake Michigan with the weather deteriorating and winds blowing at up to 35 mph. The *Bradley* had prepared for severe weather by securing its hatch covers along with its unloading boom. Also, Captain Bryan elected to take the route along the lee of the Wisconsin shore offering some protection from the storm.

Overnight, the wind increased into a full gale with waves whipped into whitecaps. Winds reached gusts up to 60 mph and the swells were 20 feet high. The *Bradley* plowed ahead in these heavy seas, and because she had no cargo, took on additional water ballast. This allowed the vessel to ride smoothly, without strain. By the afternoon of November 18, the *Bradley* altered her course heading towards Lansing Shoal at the top of Lake Michigan. The wind had increased to 65 mph and the wave crests were reaching 20 feet high, but the vessel was working well in the seas. She was twisting and hogging through the storm, but bulk carriers like the *Bradley* were designed to be flexible.

At 5:15 pm, Captain Bryan radioed the Bradley Transportation Line at Roger City that the vessel was to arrive 2:00 am. The crew was still in high spirits, looking forward to arriving home in a few hours. At 5:31 pm, the first mate, Elmer Fleming, and Captain Bryan heard a large thud astern. The two spun around in the pilothouse looking towards the stern and noticed it sagging. Seconds later, another thud was heard, as the bow heaved upward and the stern sagged still lower. Captain Bryan recognized that the *Bradley* was breaking up, and ordered Fleming to send out distress signals. Fleming yelled out, "Mayday!" on the radiophone. As he repeated his message, the Marine Radio Station at Port Washington, Wisconsin, received the message. The radioman ordered the channel cleared as Fleming's voice echoed out again, "Mayday! Mayday! Mayday! This is the *Carl D. Bradley*. Our position is approximately 12 miles southwest of Gull Island. We are in serious trouble."

While Fleming was speaking another voice yelled out, "Run, grab life jackets! Get your life jackets!"

As Captain Bryan and Elmer Fleming were requesting help, a third thud echoed through the vessel. The fore and aft sections began to separate. At 5:45 pm, Fleming gave a final plea over the radiophone, "The ship is breaking up in heavy seas. We're breaking up. We're going to sink. We're going down! Mayday! Mayday! Mayday!"

Before Fleming finished, a fourth and final thud reverberated throughout the vessel and the electrical lines to the bow section were severed. The *Bradley* heaved upward near the No. 10 hatch and broke in two, the two sections quickly starting to sink. Surrounded by churning waves, both sections began to list heavily. Men scrambled to the high side, but before anyone could react, the forward section lurched over, spilling everyone into the water. Luckily, several crewmen on the forward section were able to pull out a stored liferaft. Frank Mays, a deck watchman, surfaced from the waters within arm's length of the liferaft. Mays heard another crewman yelling towards him from the raft. On board the raft was Elmer Fleming. Quickly, Fleming helped Mays onto the raft. The two men then attempted to locate other crewmen amid the waves. Through the darkness, Gary Strezlecki called out to them. Fleming

LEFT: The *Francisco Morazon* stranded on Lake Michigan, the crew clambering down the side of the ship into a small boat.

and Mays struggled to get him out of the water, and eventually were able to pull him aboard. Another voice moaned out nearby. It was Dennis Meredith, another mate, who had been sleeping when the alarm rang out. Meredith quickly ran out on deck clad only in light clothing. When he was pulled aboard the raft, Meredith was already suffering from exposure. His face was a grayish-blue and he had trouble staying coherent.

The men on the stern section were not so fortunate. The two lifeboats could not be launched since the steep angle of the deck prevented it. The crewmen held onto the railing. Hoping the life jackets they wore would keep them alive long enough until rescue would arrive. Eventually, the stern section dove under the waves. The icy water came into contact with the hot boilers in the Bradley's engine room and the boilers exploded. The four men on the raft, along with a nearby steamer, the *Christian Sartori*, sighted the flash from the explosion.

The four men on the liferaft waited for rescue. Fleming located the survival kit which included some flares, and quickly fired them off. The steamer *Sartori* spotted the flares, but in the severe weather it would take another hour before the *Sartori* could reach the area. After searching, the captain of the *Sartori* radioed stating that no lifeboats were found and he believed all hands were lost. Other vessels led by the Coast Guard Cutter *Sundew* and several aircraft continued the search throughout the night.

On the liferaft, the men struggled to stay alive. The raft consisted of several planks mounted over sealed oil drums. It offered little protection from the biting cold and the fury of the storm. Several times waves crashed over the raft flipping it over and sending the men into the water. One time the raft flipped end over end, but only two men were able to hold on to the raft, Mays and Fleming—Meredith and Strezlecki disappeared under the waves.

By morning of November 19, an aircraft spotted the liferaft. The cutter *Sundew* pulled Fleming and Mays aboard. They would be the only survivors. The Coast Guard recovered 17 bodies along with an overturned lifeboat. None of the men on watch in the engine room were among the bodies recovered.

The investigation on the loss of the *Carl D. Bradley* cited several reasons for the disasters, but most of the blame was focused on Captain Bryan. Investigators stated that Captain Bryan had exercised poor judgment for proceeding across northern Lake Michigan instead of waiting for better conditions. Another theory regarding to the loss of the *Bradley* was that the

hull had some defect or hairline cracks. However, the direct cause has yet to be determined. The mystery of why the *Bradley* broke up still remains unsolved.

Owner: United States Steel Corporation
Builder: American Shipbuilding Company
Dimensions: 623.0 x 65.0 x 33.0, 10,028 gt.
Built: 1927 at Lorain, Ohio

Francisco Morazan

November 23, 1960
Lake Michigan

In blinding snow and 40 mph winds, the *Francisco Morazan* lost its bearings on Lake Michigan. Suddenly, the *Morazan* shuttered to a stop. She had run hard aground off South Manitou Island. The *Morazan* had left Chicago ignoring gale warnings on November 23, 1960. The steamer was attempting to reach the "Soo" before the locks closed for the season. The *Francisco Morazan* was declared a total loss, but no lives were lost.

Owner: Moa Naviera S. A.
Builder: Deutsche Werft A. G.
Dimensions: 246.9 x 36.1 x 16.8, 1,412 gt.
Built: 1922 at Hamburg, Germany

Cedarville

May 7, 1965
Lake Huron

BELOW: The self unloading steamer *Cedarville* sank after being struck by the Norwegian freighter *Topalsfjord* in 1965.

Dense fog resulted in the lost of the self-unloading steel steamer *Cedarville* on May 7, 1965. The *Cedarville* collided with the Norwegian freighter *Topdalsfjord* a mile east of the Mackinac Bridge. The *Cedarville* was a mile away when both vessels veered and changed course. At that point, the master of the *Topdalsfjord* thought the two vessels would pass each other on the starboard side. However, a miscommunication prevented him from hearing a

LEFT: The steamer *Daniel J. Morrell* unexpectedly broke in two on Lake Huron in 1966. Only one crewman, Dennis Hale, survived.

Cedarville message that said she was going hard to port to bring his vessel across his bow. Not until the bow of the *Topdalsfjord* was within feet of the *Cedarville* did either master realize the collision would occur. Both vessels were equipped with radar, which should have prevented the disaster. A Coast Guard hearing noted that poor verbal communications between the vessels led to disaster. Ten of the *Cedarville* crewmen were lost.

Owner: United States Steel Corporation
Builder: Great Lakes Engineering Works
Dimensions: 588.3 x 60.2 x 30.8, 8,575 gt.
Built: 1927 at River Rouge, Michigan

Daniel J. Morrell

November 26, 1966
Lake Erie

On November 26, 1966, the *Daniel J. Morrell* was heading down Lake Erie towards Buffalo on her last trip of the season. Before arriving at Buffalo, New York, a radio call was received. Due to a breakdown of another vessel, the *Morrell* would make one more trip up to Taconite Harbor, Minnesota.

Arriving at Buffalo, the *Morrell* sat in line waiting to be unloaded. Several crewmen decided to make a quick trip home. Dennis Hale, a deck watchman, kept a car at the Bethlehem Steel dock, so he and John Groh, another watchman, headed to their homes. After Hale dropped Groh off at his home in Erie, Pennsylvania, he headed for his house in Ashtabula, Ohio. The next day the two returned to Buffalo, New York, but arrived only in time to see the *Morrell* steaming out of the harbor. Hale hurried over to the nearby Coast Guard station and radioed to the *Morrell*. After a brief discussion with Captain Crawley, it was decided that Hale and Groh would meet up with the vessel at Mullin's Fuel Dock near Windsor, Ontario.

The *Morrell* headed up Lake Erie as it had done numerous times before. It was snowing and a fresh wind was blowing, but the *Morrell* was riding well. The steamer was a bit higher out of the water since it left Buffalo with only ballast. As she reached the entrance to the Detroit River, Captain Crawley received word of adverse weather approaching. Crawley discussed the situation with Captain Connelly, the master of the *Edward Y. Townsend*. The two

RIGHT: A view of the *Daniel J. Morrell* proceeding up light. When the *Morrell* was lost, it was also proceeding up light with no cargo only ballast.

discussed whether to proceed or wait for better conditions. Both decided to wait. The *Townsend* dropped anchor on Lake St. Clair while the *Morrell* anchored on Lake Erie near the Detroit River.

On the morning of November 28, the *Morrell* headed up the Detroit River and continued on to the fuel dock off Windsor. They had been waiting nearly 12 hours, but conditions seemed not to improve. However, Captain Crawley now had two of his missing watchmen, Hale and Groh, who had been waiting at the fuel dock. The vessel took on an additional 221 tons of coal and departed up through the St. Clair River. After traveling a short distance, Captain Crawley was still uncertain about the weather and decided to wait a few more hours. After another discussion between Crawley and Connelly, they realized that the weather was getting worse and the two vessels would just have to continue on.

By early evening, as the *Morrell* and the *Townsend* headed up Lake Huron, the bad weather had developed into a full storm. The vessels groaned under the strain of the waves washing over the decks. Neither showed any sign that it was in any danger, and both captains were maintained radio contact reporting on weather and conditions.

At 10:00 pm, Captain Connelly clocked the wind speed at 50 mph with the waves reaching 12 feet high. He considered heading back to the shelter of the St. Clair River, but it would require a dangerous turn into the trough of the waves. Connelly elected to keep his vessel pointed directly into the storm. Captain Crawley experienced similar conditions on the *Morrell*. Down below deck, the forward crewmen tried to get some rest, but the shuddering rise and fall of the *Morrell*'s bow with each wave, made sleep difficult.

Around 2:00 am, a large thud echoed through the *Morrell*. A large fissure appeared along the port side of the deck near the No. 11 hatch. Before anyone could react, the crack grew larger. Arcs of blue light flashed as the electric wires broke. Steam pipes burst as the *Morrell* began to twist apart. The forward section lost power, including the power to the radio-telephone. The *Morrell* was about to break in two and no distress signal could be sent.

The crew on watch and those who had been sleeping, quickly reacted to their situation. Those below deck gathered up on deck in various stages of dress, but most had their life jackets. The men gathered around the liferaft, which was designed to hold fifteen men—not all the crew could get aboard. Some waited quietly, while others asked what had caused the vessel to breakup. However, there was no panic among the men as each prepared for the impending ordeal.

About 15 minutes after the crack first appeared, the bow section tore away completely from the rest of the ship. With the cargo hold open to the seas, the bow section quickly settled lower as water rushed in. Waves smashed against the hull swinging the bow section sideways.

The forward crew watched in horror as the stern section headed directly towards them. Just as the stern approached, the bow swung far enough away that the stern passed to the side of the nearly submerged bow. It continued on its way under its own power into the distance. Shortly afterwards, the bow lurched skywards hurling the raft and its occupants into the water.

When the men surfaced again among the waves, only a few remained near the raft. There was John Cleary and Art Stojek, who were deckhands, along with watchman Dennis Hale. The three men looked around for any other survivors and caught sight of wheelsman, Charles Fosbender. Quickly they pulled him aboard, but they did not see anyone else in the water.

Hale and Cleary took charge on the raft. They opened a storage compartment and retrieved several hand flares along with a flashlight. Fosbender took the flashlight and began waving it back and forth toward some distance lights. When Hale asked what he was doing, Fosbender pointed out the lights and said he was trying to signal the nearby vessel. Then the men realized that the lights were from the stern section of the *Morrell*! It had continued on its way for several miles under its own power.

The four men struggled to stay warm on the raft. Hale was dressed in shorts and a pea coat. Stojek was dressed only slightly better, wearing lightweight pajamas. Cleary and Fosbender were fully dressed. The men clung to the raft as the frigid wind and spray from the waves froze over their drenched bodies. All they could do was pray for an end to their ordeal.

On the morning of November 29, the storm abated, giving some relief to the men, but the rising sun overhead offered little warmth in the extreme cold of November. When Hale and Fosbender awoke, they discovered that Cleary and Stojek had perished during the night. The two surviving men spoke very little, but tried to keep themselves as warm as possible. Later that afternoon, Hale tried talking to Fosbender again, but Fosbender started coughing heavily. A few moments later Fosbender died. His chest and shoulders had been crushed when the vessel had gone down. Dennis Hale found himself alone on the liferaft; though he did not know it, no search was to begin for another 20 hours.

At 2:00 pm, Captain Connelly contacted Bethlehem reporting the condition of the *Townsend*. He stated that his gyroscope was out and he was holding into the wind at the top of Lake Huron. Connelly said he had last heard from the *Morrell* at 12:15 am, and that it should be some 15 miles ahead of her. The Bethlehem dispatcher contacted another vessel in the fleet, the *Arthur B. Homer*, and asked its captain to watch for the *Morrell*. Both vessels attempted to contact the *Morrell*, but they assumed that the storm must have knocked out its antenna. By evening, no vessel had sighted the *Morrell* or was able to contact her. At the Bethlehem offices, there grew great concern over its overdue vessel. The company put an urgent call to the Coast Guard to begin a search.

The Coast Guard put out an alert to all vessels on Lake Huron to watch for the missing *Morrell*. An hour later, a freighter came upon some wreckage off Harbor Beach, Michigan. The wreckage consisted of several life rings, oil cans, and three bodies face down in the water. The Coast Guard focused its search to the area where the wreckage was found. As more bodies were discovered, hope of finding survivors dwindled.

Dennis Hale still lay across the raft when the last rays of light left the sky. He was alone on the liferaft next to three of his dead shipmates. The hours of exposure to the elements had taken the little strength he had. Hale was in pain, but all he could was endure until rescue arrived. During the night, the raft grounded on some offshore rocks near the shoreline. Hale knew he was no more than a few feet from solid ground, but he was too weak to move. He glanced over and caught sight of a nearby farmhouse. Hale yelled out hoping someone would hear him, but the roar of the waves muffled his screams. Several hours later, snow began to fall making matters worse.

Throughout the morning and afternoon of November 30, Dennis Hale was near death. He was suffering from hypothermia and ice had formed around his jacket. Hale also began to eat the ice off his jacket, but soon stopped. Had he continued, the ice would have lowered his body temperature and most likely he would have died. At 4:00 pm, Dennis Hale heard the sound of two Coast Guard helicopters circling overhead. They had spotted the liferaft, but assumed that all four men had already expired. When Hale raised his arm, the crew realized there was a survivor.

Dennis Hale was the sole survivor of the loss of the *Daniel J. Morrell*. None of the crew on the stern section survived. It is believed that the crew on the stern attempted to launch a lifeboat, but discovered that the conditions on Lake Huron prevented it. Also, the crew knew that when the stern sank, the icy water would come into contact with the boilers causing them to explode. Without any other choices, they probably jumped into the lake with only the aid of their life jackets. Eventually, the men would have succumbed to hypothermia or drowned amid the storm-tossed waves.

The reason for the loss of the *Morrell* was quickly discovered. When the steamer *Edward Y. Townsend* reached the St. Mary's River, its crew discovered a large crack across its deck. The two vessels were nearly identical and had experienced similar conditions. The cracks on decks of the *Townsend* and *Morrell* resulted from a structural failure in the hull girder amidships. After the loss, older ships were required to have structural strengthening. Additional recommendations were made by investigators to have better lifesaving devices, but this was small consolation to those families of the 28 men who perished on the *Daniel J. Morrell*.

Owner: Bethlehem Steel Corporation
Builder: West Bay City Shipbuilding
Dimensions: 265.0 x 38.2 x 19.5, 1,961 gt.
Built: 1903 at Port Huron, Michigan

Meteor

November 21, 1969
Lake Superior

BELOW: The whaleback steamer *Meteor* shown here after its conversion to a tanker. The *Meteor* ended its career when it grounded on Lake Superior.

The whaleback steamer *Meteor* met disaster twice on Lake Superior. While sailing under the name *Frank Rockefeller*, the steamer crashed ashore on November 2, 1905, off Isle Royale. The steamer and her tow were lost in a blinding snowstorm when it struck the shallow waters off the island. However, most of the damage from the grounding resulted from the barge in tow. When the *Rockefeller* hit the rocks, the barge behind her kept on moving until it crashed into the stern of the *Rockefeller*. The whaleback's stern was crushed and its hull holed, but it was repaired and put back into service.

By 1969, the *Rockefeller* had been sold to Cleveland Tankers, renamed *Meteor*, and converted into a tanker. On November 21, 1969, the *Meteor* ran aground on Gull Island Shoal off Marquette, Michigan. The damage was severe and required extensive repairs to the hull. In addition, the *Meteor* was a single-hull tanker. The environmental impact of oil spill on the lakes warranted the *Meteor* to be retired. Since she was the last surviving whaleback, she was salvaged, repaired, and now serves as a museum vessel at Superior, Wisconsin.

Owner: Pittsburgh Steamship Company, Cleveland Tankers
Builder: American Steel Barge Company
Dimensions: 366.0 x 45.0 x 25.0, 2,759 gt.
Built: 1896 at West Superior, Wisconsin

Eastcliffe Hall

July 14, 1970
St. Lawrence River

On July 14, 1970, the steel motor vessel *Eastcliffe Hall* proceeded down the St. Lawrence River with a cargo of pig iron. Around 4:00 am, she struck a shoal and sank within minutes. The crew on duty was able to escape, but nine men were trapped below deck and perished. A Canadian Court of Inquiry investigated the tragedy and cited the master and the mates responsible. The master was known for his drinking and was intoxicated when his vessel sank.

Owner: Hall Corporation
Builder: Canadian Vickers Ltd.
Dimensions: 343.4 x 43.8 x 22.8, 3,335 gt.
Built: 1954 at Montreal, Quebec

Edmund Fitzgerald

November 10, 1975
Lake Erie

On June 8, 1958, the *Edmund Fitzgerald* was christened to fresh water. More than 10,000 people watched the gala event as the *Fitzgerald* splashed majestically into the water. With 729 feet of new steel along its keel, the *Fitzgerald* was the largest vessel yet to venture out on the inland seas. She was given the label, "Pride of the American Flag," the ore carrier was destined for a successful long career. The *Fitzgerald* was the start of a new era of transportation on the Great Lakes. Northwestern Mutual Life, the first insurance company to invest in a Great Lakes vessel, owned the *Edmund Fitzgerald*. The company charted out its vessel to Oglebay Norton for 25 years. Under Oglebay Norton's care, the *Fitzgerald* broke various shipping records on the Great Lakes. In 1964, the *Fitzgerald* carried over a million gross tons of ore through the "Soo." In 1968, the ore carrier topped its mark by another 200,000 tons, setting an even higher record. In 1969, the *Fitzgerald* carried over 27,400 tons of ore in her holds marking the largest single load.

Early afternoon of November 9, 1975, the *Edmund Fitzgerald* finished loading 26,116 long tons of taconite pellets at the Burlington Northern Railroad Dock at Superior, Wisconsin. It was a warm clear November day. Everything was routine, deckhands were busily covering the 21 separate hatch covers. Each hatch required 68 clamps to be manually tightened to secure it. By 2:00 pm, all the hatch covers were secured and the *Fitzgerald* proceeded out into Lake Superior. In command was Captain Earnest McSorley. McSorley was

a veteran sailor and knew his vessel well. He began his career at sea as an 18-year old deck-hand on ocean freighters. When he took command of the *Fitzgerald*, he had over 44 years of experience behind him.

Two hours later, the *Arthur M. Anderson* left Two Harbors also carrying a cargo of taconite bound for Gary, Indiana. Her master, Jesse B. Cooper, sighted the *Fitzgerald* on the horizon. He heard security reports coming from Superior, Wisconsin, of the *Fitzgerald*'s departure. Captain Cooper also received weather reports of small craft warnings. By 7:00 pm, the National Weather Service released gale warnings; after midnight, another weather report escalated to storm warnings. Captain Cooper of the *Anderson* radioed Captain McSorley of the *Fitzgerald* about the worsening weather. The forecast projected winds reaching upward of 60 mph. After a brief discussion, the two captains agreed to sail along the protective northern route of the Canadian shore.

For the next six hours, the *Fitzgerald* and the *Anderson* proceeded along similar courses. The route would taken them toward Michipicoten Island, then take a turn south past Caribou Island, and finally into the safety of Whitefish Bay. The *Fitzgerald* was the faster of the two and pulled some 10 miles ahead of the *Anderson*. Both vessels seem to be riding smoothly, in spite of the increasing strength of the sea.

In the afternoon of November 10, the *Fitzgerald* and *Anderson* altered their course to pass Caribou Island and Six Fathom Shoal. Watching the *Fitzgerald* on radar, Captain Cooper was concerned about how close she was getting to the shoal—something that Captain McSorley could not see because the *Fitzgerald* carried no fathometer or depth gauge to determine the depth of water. On the *Fitzgerald*, to judge depth, the crew had to use an old-fashioned hand lead that required a man to stand out on the bow and throw a line with a weight overboard. In normal conditions, this was a simple process, but the *Fitzgerald* was in the middle of a Lake Superior storm! No man dared ventured out on deck for he would be washed overboard.

Around 4:00 pm, the *Fitzgerald* contacted another vessel, the *Avafors*, a Swedish saltwater vessel, and asked if the radio beacon and light at Whitefish Point were in operation. The *Avafors*' pilot reported that the light could not been seen and the radio beacon was not broadcasting. McSorley learned later from the Coast Guard that the station at Whitefish Point had a power failure and nothing was operational. He then radioed the *Anderson* that his vessel had lost both its radars and he needed some help with navigation. Both vessels were in winds of over 65 mph and waves reaching 18 feet. Snow continued to fall, making visibility between difficult. The *Fitzgerald* called once an hour to get an update on her position.

An hour later, the *Avafors*' pilot contacted the *Fitzgerald* about the radio beacon. The pilot was able to talk directly with Captain McSorley and mentioned that the beacon was still not broadcasting. The two talked for a short time before McSorley mentioned that the *Fitzgerald* "had a bad list, had lost both radars, and was taking heavy seas over the deck." McSorley continued to say that the storm was one of the worst he had ever experienced.

By 6:00 pm, the two vessels had passed by Caribou Island. The first mate on the *Anderson* kept a close eye on the radar screen watching for the *Fitzgerald*. Waves smashed over the ore carrier's pilothouse sending a wall of water careening down the length of deck. The *Anderson* recorded waves as high as 25 feet. At 7:10 pm, the first mate on the *Anderson* contacted the *Fitzgerald*. He told them of the vessels nine miles ahead that were going to pass the *Fitzgerald* to the west. The mate asked how the *Fitzgerald* was handling in the storm, and the *Fitzgerald* replied, "We are holding our own." Captain Cooper returned to the pilothouse just as the mate finished his conversation with the *Fitzgerald*. The two officers took another view at the radar, noting the *Fitzgerald* was about nine miles ahead and 14 miles off Whitefish Point. This was the last time anyone would see the *Fitzgerald* on radar.

Shortly afterward, the snow stopped falling and the visibility improved. From the pilot-house of the *Anderson*, several lights were visible. One red light could be clearly seen from shore. Another set of lights—from the saltwater vessels heading out of Whitefish Bay—was spotted by the first mate. The wheelsman spotted a single white light in the distance, but no one else in the pilothouse could see it. Captain Cooper was concerned that no one could see the lights from the *Fitzgerald*. He went over to the radar, but only the saltwater vessels were visible. Next, he tried to contact the *Fitzgerald* by radio, but there was no response. Greatly

ABOVE: The steamer *Edmund Fitzgerald* with a cargo of iron ore.

alarmed, he attempted to reach the Coast Guard at Sault Ste. Marie, but it would take another hour before he could make contact—around 8:30 pm. Cooper told the Coast Guard that he lost track of the *Fitzgerald*. While he tried to explain his concerns, the Coast Guard alerted the *Anderson* of a missing small boat in the area. Cooper was more concerned about a missing 729 foot vessel! Eventually, the Coast Guard began confirming Cooper's report. They were not able to contact the *Fitzgerald* either.

At 9:15 pm, the Coast Guard dispatched a search aircraft and notified the Canadian Rescue Center that an ore carrier had disappeared on Lake Superior. By 9:30 pm, the Coast Guard cutter *Naugatuck,* stationed at Sault Ste. Marie, received orders to search for the *Fitzgerald*, but it couldn't set sail until the following morning because an oil line breakage needed repair. The Coast Guard also ordered the buoy tender *Woodrush*—stationed at Duluth, and so 24 hours away—to search for the *Fitzgerald*. .

With its own vessels having difficulty reaching the search area, the Coast Guard contacted freighters to help in the search. After contacting seven vessels, only the *William Clay Ford* and the *Hilda Marjanne* were willing to help. The *Hilda Marjanne* was driven back to the shelter of Whitefish Bay, but the *Ford* joined the *Anderson* in the search. Eventually, six other vessels assisted, but it was futile. The *Edmund Fitzgerald* had gone down somewhere on Lake Superior.

The morning of November 11 confirmed the *Fitzgerald's* fate. The *Anderson* located a section of the ore carrier's lifeboat. Shortly afterwards, the steamer *William R. Roesch* discovered another lifeboat. It had been mangled and a large portion had sheered off. The motor vessel *Roger Blough* found an inflatable liferaft, but there were no signs of it ever being occupied. Other pieces of wreckage were discovered through out the day. The flotsam included oars, a sounding board, propane tanks, life rings, and several other small objects from the *Fitzgerald*. However, there were no bodies found.

On November 14, a Navy aircraft was able to locate the sunken remains of the *Fitzgerald*, but it wouldn't be until next spring before a submersible vehicle was able to make an underwater survey of the wreckage. It photographed two large sections in 530 feet of water. The bow section, some 276 feet long, was resting upright, while the stern section, around 170 feet long, was upside down. Scattered between the two sections were torn hull plates and the *Fitzgerald's* cargo of iron ore.

An investigation was immediately started to find out what had caused the *Fitzgerald* to suddenly founder. After reviewing statements from the *Anderson's* crew and studying the underwater photographs, investigators provided their findings in 1977. They concluded that the *Fitzgerald* had foundered due to the loss of sufficient freeboard due to flooding of the cargo holds. They concluded that several cargo hold hatches had failed during the storm allowing water to enter into the holds.

While investigators had determined the proximate cause of the loss of the *Fitzgerald*, there were many others who remained skeptical. Captain Cooper of the *Anderson* was convinced that the reason for the *Fitzgerald*'s demise was that the vessel had struck the shoals off Caribou Island. He concluded that the damage from grounding caused the vessel to sink afterward. The Lake Carriers' Association, who also concluded that the *Fitzgerald* hit a shoal causing the vessel to sink, backed his theory. Other historians offer various other theories including that the *Fitzgerald* broke in two or capsized. However, no one is certain of the exact cause, and although a great deal of information has been gathered, the mystery of the *Edmund Fitzgerald* still lingers today.

ABOVE: The steel steamer *Frontenac* was a constructive loss after striking a reef in 1979. The steamer was one of five vessels to use the name *Frontenac*.

Owner: Northwestern Mutual Life Insurance Company
Builder: Great Lakes Engineering
Dimensions: 729.0 x 75.0 x 39.0, 13,632 gt.
Built: 1958 at River Rouge, Michigan.

Frontenac

November 22, 1979
Lake Superior

The *Frontenac* was heading into Silver Bay, Lake Superior, with a cargo of bunker fuel when a snow squall dropped visibility to zero. The weather also knocked out her radar, and minutes later, the *Frontenac* struck Pellet Island Reef, sustained severe damage, and began to take on water. The Coast Guard responded quickly, placing an oil containment boom around the vessel. The *Frontenac* had extensive damage to over 300 feet of her hull, but was freed and towed to Superior, Wisconsin. After inspection, she was declared a total loss and sold for scrap.

Owner: Cleveland Cliffs Steamship Company
Builder: Great Lakes Engineering Works
Dimensions: 590.0 x 60.0 x 27.8, 8,158 gt.
Built: 1923 at River Rouge, Michigan

Mesquite

December 4, 1989
Lake Superior

On December 4, 1989, the Coast Guard cutter *Mesquite* was busily pulling navigation buoys from Lake Superior. Normally, she would be working along Lake Michigan, but her sister vessel, the *Sundew*, was in dry-dock at Sturgeon Bay, Wisconsin. The *Mesquite* had to work double duty before the winter freezing prevented it. Around 1:00 am, the *Mesquite* sailed to the tip of the Keweenaw Peninsula. After it picked up a buoy, the cutter pulled away a short distance and struck hard aground—the officers on board had failed to plot their exact location. Before the cutter could be salvaged, storms damaged the *Mesquite* beyond repair. The following July, she was lifted a short distance and sunk to be part of an underwater preserve.

Owner: United States Coast Guard
Builder: Marine Iron and Shipbuilding Company
Dimensions: 180.0 x 37.0 x 12.0, 1,025 gt.
Built: 1942 at Duluth, Minnesota

Algolake

September 23, 1994
St. Lawrence River

The steel motor vessel *Algolake* damaged its propeller on December 28, 1983, while entering Thunder Bay, Ontario. On April 3, 1985, combustible materials caught fire in the engineroom while the steamer was traveling down the St. Clair River. Although the crew limited the fire, the *Algolake* was forced to run aground on Lake St. Clair. Then, on September 23, 1994, the vessel ran aground again, this time on the St. Lawrence River—the pilot *Algolake* was unaware of a buoy displacement on the river and navigated the vessel into shallow waters.

BELOW: The modern 730-foot *Algolake* had an engine room fire in 1985. Notice the absence of a pilothouse.

Owner: Algoma Central Railway
Builder: Collingwood Shipyard
Dimensions: 730.0 x 75.0 x 46.5, 22,852 gt.
Built: 1976 at Collingwood, Ontario

Appendix 1: Alphabetical Listing of Wrecks on the Great Lakes

NAME	TYPE	HOW	YEAR
Adella Shores	Steamer	Foundered	1909
Admiral	Tugboat	Foundered	1942
Albany	Steamer	Collided with *Philadelphia* and sank off Point aux Barques	1893
Algolake	Freighter	Run aground in St Lawrence River	1994
Algoma	Steamer	Stranded on Isle Royale	1885
Alpena	Paddle Steamer	Probably foundered	1880
America	Steamer	Struck reef out of Washington Harbor	1928
Ann Arbor No. 1	Ferry	Burned at Manitowoc, Wisconsin	1910
Anna C. Minch	Steamer	Foundered in storm off Ludington	1940
Annie M. Peterson	Barge	Driven ashore during storm	1914
Argus	Steamer	Foundered on Lake Huron	1913
Arlington	Steamer	Flooded and sank south of Superior Shoal	1940
Armenia	Barge	Foundered near Pelee Island Light	1906
Asia	Steamer	Foundered on Lake Huron	1882
Aycliffe Hall	Steamer	Collided with *Edward J. Berwind* and sank, Lake Erie	1936
Azov	Schooner	Foundered on Lake Huron	1911
Bannockburn	Steamer	Vanished on Lake Superior	1902
C. F. Curtis	Steamer	Driven aground during storm	1914
Carl D. Bradley	Steamer	Broke up and sank on Lake Michigan	1958
Cedarville	Steamer	Collision with *Topdalsfjord* in Straits of Mackinac	1965
Charles S. Price	Steamer	Foundered during storm on Lake Huron	1913
Choctaw	Steamer	Collided with Wacondah on Lake Huron	1915
City of Bangor	Steamer	Ran ashore off Keweenaw Point	1926
City of Green Bay	Schooner	Flooded and sank on Lake Michigan	1887
City of Port Huron	Ferry	Sank at dock	1939
Cleveco	Oil Tank Barge	Foundered on Lake Erie	1942
Clifton	Whaleback	Foundered on Lake Erie	1924
Cyprus	Steamer	Flooded, capsized, and sank 18 miles north of Deer Park, west of Whitefish Point	1907
D. M. Clemson	Steamer	Flooded while storm damaged	1908
Daniel J. Morrell	Steamer	Broke in two during a storm	1966
David Dows	Schooner	Foundered on Lake Michigan	1889
Delaware	Propellor	Storm damaged and stranded	1855
Eastcliffe Hall	Freighter	Collided with reef and sank	1970
Eastland	Steamer	Scrapped after capsizing in dock	1915
Edmund Fitzgerald	Freighter	Sank about 17 miles north by northwest of Whitefish Point	1975
Emperor	Steamer	Stranded and sank on Canoe Rocks Reef, Isle Royale	1947
Erie Belle	Tug	Exploded at Kidcardine	1883
Francisco Morazon	Steamer	Grounded on Lake Michigan	1960
Frontenac	Steamer	Grounded on Lake Superior	1979
George M. Cox	Steamer	Ran aground on Rock of Ages reef	1933
Glenlyon	Steamer	Struck a reef and flooded	1924
Globe	Steamer/Barge	Exploded/Caught fire	1860/73

NAME	TYPE	HOW	YEAR
Griffon	Ketch	Disappeared	1679
Gunilda	Steel Steam Yacht	Sank after running aground	1911
Henry B. Smith	Steamer	Foundered on Lake Superior	1913
Henry Steinbrenner	Steamer	Foundered off Isle Royale	1953
Howard M. Hanna, Jr.	Steel Steamer	Stranded during a storm	1913
Hydrus	Steamer	Foundered during a storm	1913
Idaho	Steamer	Foundered off Long Point, Lake Erie	1897
Iosco	Steamer	Foundered during a storm	1905
Ira H. Owen	Steamer	Foundered during a storm	1905
Isaac M. Scott	Steamer	Foundered during a storm	1913
James Carruthers	Steamer	Foundered on Lake Huron	1913
John A. McGean	Steamer	Sank off Tawas Point, Lake Huron	1913
John B. Merrill	Schooner	Grounded on Holdridge Shoal	1893
L. R. Doty	Propeller	Foundered on Lake Michigan during a storm	1898
Lady Elgin	Steamer	Collided with *Augusta* and sank	1860
Lafayette	Propellor	Collided with *Manila* on Lake Superior	1905
Lambton	Lighthouse Tender	Vanished on Lake Superior	1922
Leafield	Steamer	Sank after being stranded	1913
Lizzie A. Law	Schooner	Stranded off Huron Island, Lake Superior	1908
M. I. Wilcox	Schooner	Foundered off Colchester, Ontario, Lake Erie	1906
Madeira	Barge	Stranded near Split Rock Point, Lake Superior	1905
Manistee	Propellor	Foundered on Lake Superior	1883
Marquette & Bessemer No. 2	Ferry	Foundered on Lake Erie	1909
Mataafa	Steamer	Storm damaged and stranded outside the Duluth Ship Canal	1905
Mesquite	Coast Guard Cutter	Stranded off Keweenaw Point	1989
Meteor	Whaleback Tanker	Stranded off Marquette Gull Island Shoal	1969
Minnedosa	Schooner Barge	Foundered during a storm	1905
Monarch	Freighter	Sank after striking Blake's Point	1906
Monkshaven	Propellor	Stranded south side of Angus Island, near Thunder Bay	1905
Myron	Steamer	Flooded and sank on Lake Superior	1906
Neebing	Steamer	Boiler explosion	1937
Neshoto	Steamer	Ran aground off Crisp Point	1908
Noronic	Steamer	Burned at Toronto, Ontario	1949
Northwest	Schooner	Hit submerged ice and sank	1898
Olive Jeanette	Schooner Barge	Foundered on Lake Superior	1905
Our Son	Schooner	Foundered during a storm on Lake Michigan	1930
Pere Marquette No. 3	Ferry	Damaged by ice and sank on Lake Michigan	1920
Pere Marquette No. 4	Ferry	Collided with *Pere Marquette No. 17*	1923
Pere Marquette No. 18	Ferry	Sprang a leak and sank on Lake Michigan	1910
Phoenix	Propeller	Burned on Lake Michigan	1847
Planet	Steamer	Foundered near Eagle River, Lake Superior	1863
Plymouth	Barge	Foundered on Lake Michigan during a storm	1913
Pretoria	Schooner Barge	Foundered during a gale on Lake Superior	1905

ABOVE: A view from the stern of steamer *Pere Marquette No. 3* trapped in the ice. The steamer sank slowly so everything aboard worth saving was taken off before it finally went down. (See page 92)

NAME	TYPE	HOW	YEAR
Racine	Propellor	Sank off Point Pelee, Ontario, Lake Erie	1864
Regina	Steamer	Foundered during a storm on Lake Huron	1913
Rouse Simmons	Schooner	Sank on Lake Michigan during a storm	1912
Scotiadoc	Steamer	Collision with *Burlington*, Lake Superior	1953
Selden E. Marvin	Schooner Barge	Stranded offshore on Lake Superior	1914
Sevona	Steamer	Storm damage, stranded at Sand Island Reef	1905
Superior City	Steamer	Collided with *Willis L. King* on Lake Superior	1920
Tashmoo	Steamer	Grounded on Detroit River	1936
Three Brothers	Steamer	Beached on South Manitou Island, Lake Michigan	1911
Tioga	Steamer	Exploded at dock	1919
Turret Crown	Steamer	Stranded on Manitoulin Island	1924
Two Fannies	Schooner	Foundered during a storm	1890
W. H. Glitcher	Steamer	Foundered on Lake Michigan	1892
Waubuno	Steamer	Struck rocks on Lake Huron and sank	1879
Wells Burt	Schooner	Foundered on Lake Michigan during a storm	1883
Western Reserve	Steamer	Broke in two on Lake Superior	1892
Wexford	Steamer	Foundered on Lake Huron during a storm	1913
Zenith City	Steamer	Stranded on Au Sable Reef	1910

Appendix 2: Diveable Wrecks on the Great Lakes

Vessel	Loran	Depth
Admiral	43808.88 / 57412.71	59' to 74'
Albany	30775.5 / 49174.2	135' to 140'
Algoma	46177.8 / 31738.3	10' to 100'
America	46082.2 / 31909.2	4' to 85'
Cedarville	31210.7 / 48130.6	40' to 106'
Charles S. Price	30799.6 / 49622.5	40' to 65'
Chester A. Congdon	46147.8 / 31717.5	70' to 110'
Clarion	43890.88 / 57297.68	58' to 77'
Emperor	46150.6 / 31711.8	30' to 130'
Francisco Morazan	31858.5 / 48339.3	0' to 20'
George M. Cox	31934.9 / 46069.8	12' to 97'
John B. Merrill	30880.28 / 48191.97	30' to 80'
Mesquite	31714.6 / 46712.8	82' to 112'
Miztec	31156.9 / 47561.2	10' to 20'
Monarch	46171.2 / 31702.5	10' to 150'
Myron	31142.9 / 47566.5	42' to 50'
Neshoto	31181.2 / 47527.4	10' to 20'
Northwest	31270.2 / 48102.2	73'
Queen of the West	43986.0 / 57735.1	60' to 71'
Regina	30801.7 / 49534.9	60' to 83'
Sagamore	31072.9 / 47771.8	42' to 63'
Sevona	32388.1 / 46032.9	16' to 20'
Three Brothers	31839.28 / 48339.32	5' to 45'
Tioga	31817.3 / 46556.3	28' to 35'
Two Fannies	43773.1 / 57385.2	51' to 61'

RIGHT: *Myron*'s ship's whistle rests at the bottom of Lake Superior.

Index